UNLEASHED!

UNLEASHED!

The C1-13 Integrative Deliverance Needs
Assessment: A Qualitative and Quantitative
Probability Indicator

PETER J. BELLINI

Forewords by

Mark Chironna
Randy Clark

WIPF & STOCK · Eugene, Oregon

UNLEASHED!
The C1-13 Integrative Deliverance Needs Assessment
A Qualitative and Quantitative Probability Indicator

Wipf & Stock
An Imprint of Wipf and Stock Publishers
199 W. 8th Ave., Suite 3
Eugene, OR 97401

www.wipfandstock.com

PAPERBACK ISBN: 978-1-5326-6137-2
HARDCOVER ISBN: 978-1-5326-6138-9
EBOOK ISBN: 978-1-5326-6139-6

Manufactured in the U.S.A.   OCTOBER 25, 2018

This small book is dedicated to the glory of God our Father, the Lord Jesus Christ, and the blessed Holy Spirit who delivers us from the power of sin and death. I also dedicate this work to my wife and best friend Maria Grazia (Mariuccia) and to my children Pietro Aaronne and Paola Arianna, and my grandaughter Costanza. They are my earthly joy, strength, and inspiration. Finally, this work is dedicated to all who the Lord desires to liberate from the bondage of evil by his incomparable power and authority.

Contents

Foreword by Dr. Mark J. Chironna

A WORLD WHERE THINGS invisible govern things visible is now accepted in quantum physics. Such a world has already been known and acknowledged by the ancients. Scripture attests that the world that is unseen is far more present than we are often consciously aware. In that unseen world, entities and forces are at play that defy purely rational thinking and rational narratives. Even within the development of modern psychology, the shift from Freud's theories about the unconscious that led to psychodynamic theory in psychology, to Skinner's behaviorism, to then the Third Force of humanistic psychology with the likes of May, Maslow, and Rogers, paved the way in therapeutic consciousness for Transpersonal Psychology, which makes room for that which is beyond consciousness and unconsciousness to include experiences that would be labeled as paranormal. Even Carl Jung, whose depth analysis gained great notoriety within therapeutic psychology, embraced encounters with a figure he claimed had the name Philemon, which, while he postulated as being simply a superior knowledge, he often consulted frequently in practices of active imagination.

Anomalies such as this are present in scientific research as well as in therapeutic clinical research. Satisfying explanations are somewhat lacking, unless we embrace a worldview that Scripture consistently speaks of where good and evil are interlocked in a cosmic battle awaiting a final and ultimate confrontation. While a world of fallen spirits that seek to harm humanity seem more a part of horror films and entertainment in the current culture, their reality is attested to in all three major monotheistic religions. A Biblical worldview acknowledges such anomalies not as mere random events, but rather as part of an entire systemic evil that is arrayed in a battle against the destiny of mankind. The Kingdom of God, established in Christ's life, death, burial, resurrection and ascension, is to be expanded through the proclamation of the Gospel under the power of the Holy Spirit, and one of the signs of the in-breaking of Christ's Kingdom is the casting out of demonic entities from the lives of those they oppress.

In a Biblical world, sin and the powers of darkness are real, and their activities and consequences in the lives of human beings is both palpable and evident. The impact of the Gospel is that it liberates human beings from the power of sin, and the oppressive powers of darkness. The casting out of such dark things is an aspect of what is known in Christian circles as the ministry of deliverance. It has its place. At the same time, Jesus approached many afflicted people and used therapeutic processes to certain situations that had nothing to do with demonic interference or the sin that so easily besets us. Some things plague us simply because we are imperfect and our flesh and blood bodies are subject to weakness and malfunctioning. In an effort to bring healing and wholeness to the suffering masses there needs to be both an awareness of demonic activity and how to address it effectively as well as therapeutic approaches to the brokenness of the human condition that have nothing to do with either sin or the powers of darkness. This is an important issue for the current culture, and especially for believers whose desire it is to facilitate healing in the lives of sufferers.

In his brand new release entitled Unleashed, Dr. Peter Bellini, from his own research and total life experience, lays the groundwork for a scholarly and sound, effective approach to the integration of the spiritual and the psychological, in addressing the demonic. With all the abuse that has taken place in many circles regarding what is referred to as "deliverance ministry," Unleashed is a gift to the saints at a time when it is deeply needed in a culture where mental illnesses are on the rise on the one hand, and occultism and new age philosophy have opened the door to a renaissance of neo-paganism, rife with gnostic dualism, and the worship of various deities other than the worship of the Triune God on the other hand. All of which leads to idolatry, which has consequences for the unrepentant that are deeply painful. Unleashed is a must-read for all those seasoned people-helpers in the Body of Christ who seek wisdom and guidance in dealing with God's people in a way that is faithful to Scripture, faithful to the Tradition (the faith once for all delivered to the saints), and faithful to true science that is free from an intellectual hubris that refuses to see what is plainly evident because it doesn't fit the narrative of an anti-Theistic worldview.

Bishop Mark J. Chironna, M.A., D Min.

Church On The Living Edge
Mark Chironna Ministries
Longwood, Florida

Foreword by Dr. Randy Clark

PETER BELLINI'S UNIQUELY-TITLED BOOK, Unleashed: The C1-13 Integrative Deliverance Needs Assessment, is a welcome addition to the field of religion dealing with demons and—the process by which we are set free from demons—deliverance. Dr. Bellini eschews simplistic characterizations of our world that would suggest every obstacle or problem is demonically rooted, providing a balanced and systematic rubric to assess deliverance needs. Bellini focuses on patient wellness and wholeness, acknowledging the benefits of modern medicine and therapy in conjunction with the supernatural. Much like Rev. John Wesley sought to use every available means at his disposal for the health and well-being of his followers, Dr. Bellini (also a Methodist) developed this tool to determine when deliverance ministry was likely warranted instead of alternative treatments.

For those on the fence regarding the existence of demons, Dr. Bellini's chapters on the theological background and supernatural worldview of demons are required reading. While defending the supernatural worldview, Bellini thankfully avoids the over sensationalism that often accompanies books on deliverance. His stories are clear, concise, and ring with honesty and authenticity. Overall it is an amazingly balanced book offering a deliverance ministry model that doesn't myopically focus on deliverance solely, but upon complete restoration and wholeness. Sometimes that wholeness happens only through deliverance ministry, more often through the normal means of grace, and sometimes—without apology—through the insights from the medical fields.

In his section on pages 51-58 titled, "Science and Religion: Friends or Foes," Bellini writes masterfully about the interplay between the two, detailing that both have their own ways of knowing, but they are not mutually exclusive. Science and Religion ask different questions. At times in the past they have been antagonistic to each other, but there are reasons to drop the antagonism and work together to find answers to the needs of human brokenness. An erudite academic, Dr. Bellini is at his best when he dawns his pastoral hat. His experience and service to the poor and broken bleeds through every page and is instructive to any potential practitioner. Dr. Bellini's model was developed while he was a pastor working in communities that were below the poverty level, who could not afford or were not aware of how to receive mental health treatment. Often his church's ministry was the major source of help to those living in its neighborhoods. In one sense, this is not a book about theory, but about a way of healing the broken and setting at liberty those who were being oppressed.

To those who diagnose every problem as demonic: read this book. To those who believe every condition is rooted in naturalistic causes: read this book. Pastors and leaders, on behalf of your community, read, consider, and put into practice these tools, which can bring healing and wholeness to those who are without hope. It is my hope that as the issue of brokenness and deliverance is acknowledged, and the good news is communicated in places of darkness, the people who set in darkness will see a great light of hope: churches empowered and equipped to set them free. Without a doubt, Dr. Bellini's work is an important tool for these churches.

Randy Clark – D. Min.

Overseer of the Apostolic Network of Global Awakening,
founder of Global Awakening

Preface

THIS SHORT WORK WAS birthed out of a larger labor of tough love inspired by a parent's inexorable drive to better care for a son's mental disorder and an urban pastor's passion to see brokenhearted people healed from sin, mental anguish, and demonic oppression. Over twenty years ago, I began to take a serious investment of time, money, research, and care in the field of mental health when I pressed my son's pediatrician to have him tested for several mental health disorders, some of which were controversial at the time but now common diagnoses. My goal was to better understand the distress that my son and others, including parishioners, were facing, as well as the nature of the burden that families and other support systems confronted when seeking to provide comfort.

With education came the hope and realization of more effective strategies and enhanced care in my ministry. I constructed a care strategy for my son as well as the oppressed in my ministry that pressed towards wholism, calling on the person and work of the Holy Spirit, natural means and measures, and a wide range of health professionals and their expertise. The cumulative result was an overall integrative approach to health and wholeness that garnered the best resources that faith and science could afford to tackle human brokenness. This integrative regimen has mitigated what was once a seemingly insurmountable charge of discerning and treating crippling distress, brokenness, and oppression. However, the problem remains vast and requires a herculean effort from a variety of sources, but what seemed once impossible is now possible.

I am an ordained Elder in the United Methodist Church and have been in ministry for over 30 years. For nearly the last decade, I have also been a Professor of Evangelization and Church Renewal at United Theological Seminary in Dayton, Ohio. During my years of ministry, I have served as a pastor, revivalist, missionary, university campus evangelist, prison minister, police chaplain, and CEO of a 501(c)(3). In my early years of ministry on a university campus and in the prison system, I recognized a call to deliverance ministry and implemented my gifting in that area. Within the first year of my radical conversion from atheism to Christ and into ministry, I evangelistically preaching in the open-air (the Oval) at the Ohio State University and in the area's prison system. In the midst of preaching to crowds and praying for students, I was soon boldly opposed by Satanists and other various groups who practiced witchcraft. I was shocked to learn that they regularly held black masses for my death and sought to cast all types of curses and spells on me to thwart and stop the ministry. I became aware of the assault when these groups openly confronted me and other colleagues and made their mission to stop us verbally clear. Much of this type of confrontation from the occult occurred in campus and urban ministry. However, pastoral issues around the collateral damage of sin, mental health, oppression, and even demonic bondage were first encountered in my ministry within the walls of the prisons.

Facing this type of formidable and consistent demonic opposition, as well as working with persons with deeply rooted mental and behavioral disorders early in my ministry, set the stage for what would become an increasingly standard caseload in my deliverance ministry. Ministering to persons with all manner of addictions, trauma, abuse, cultic and occult involvement, various mental disorders, criminal behavior, sexual brokenness, and other severe cases became the order of the day. Admittedly, early on as a charismatic revivalist, my modus operandi was more as an exorcist rather than a counselor, therapist, or one who would give a professional referral. Prescriptions of repentance and faith in Christ and/or deliverance and being filled with the Spirit were the standard remedy for such cases in those days. However, with an increasing wide variety and diversity of cases over time and a drive for effective relief and results for those whom I served, I soon realized, contra much of the literature and practice of the leading "spirit-filled" deliverance ministries, that not every spiritual problem was related to sin and/or the demonic.

I would hear numerous testimonies of relapse of those with mental disorders following deliverance sessions and claims of total cure. In my ministry, I also encountered several cases in which persons similarly relapsed after participating in deliverance sessions from other ministries and their claims of total cure. I likewise experienced comparable situations in my ministry where deliverance brought temporary symptomatic relief to some but not long-term lasting cure. I noticed that many ministries of renowned faith healers and deliverance ministers were quick to claim mental health cures with either little or no medical corroboration and rarely documentation over an extended period of time. Over such a period, symptoms may diminish or temporarily subside only to cycle and reappear later.[1]

A temporary remission of symptoms with a mental disorder does not constitute a cure. Mental disorders are complex, and manifestations can be irregular relative to various life triggers or variation in prescriptions or medication intake rhythms. Mental health and healing are best tracked by professionals over an extended period of time. Brief encounters at a healing conference or an evangelistic crusade do not provide the observation time or professional care needed to make such difficult calls. Not even a short-term follow up report a few months after a healing event by a medical professional provides substantial enough evidence and

1. An outstanding example of a healing and deliverance ministry that documents and meticulously examines all of its cases through medical professionals is Global Awakening under the leadership of Randy Clark. Global Awakening has helped establish an outside organization in concert with medical professionals and scholars from various fields entitled GMRI, the Global Medical Research Institute (globalmri.org) a 501(c)(3) for the very purpose of bringing rigorous scrutiny and medical examination to claims of healing, deliverance, and miracles in Christian ministry.

time to document a claim of curing. Pastors who have healing and deliverance ministries are able to detect this problem more acutely than healing evangelists at an event. Pastors can track the cycles of mental disorders over a period of time in conversation with the person and their doctors. They are in a more advantageous position to ascertain if there has been improvement or healing because they are with their people over a longer period of time and observe them as they walk through the various seasons of life. I became keenly aware of these insights while pastoring and ministering deliverance and healing. I was able to walk closely over time with persons who suffered from mental health issues. Along the way, I observed instances of relapse with all types of mental health issues in spite of spiritual treatment, but more apparently and intensely, I observed relapse in those with bi-polarity and schizophrenia.

Out of a compassion to see persons experience relief and the peace of God, as well as out of a professional drive to be effective and witness less relapse from my people, I began to research and incorporate a more integrative approach, as I alluded above. Also as mentioned above, the inspiration for an integrative and wholistic approach to deliverance and healing was mainly fueled by my love and treatment of my son who my wife and I had discerned through countless hours of prayer, fasting, and deliverance was not dealing with merely a sin and/or demonic issue.

As I developed a healing strategy, some of the questions and struggles I wanted resolved in my research and practice were around etiology, diagnosis, and proper treatment, thus eventually the contents of this book and the assessment instrument itself. With the complex of sinful practices and consequences, demonic strongholds, and mental and emotional disorders, how does one determine which is which, and what is the proper ministry response? For issues of sinful practice and consequence, I would let scripture properly exegeted and hermeneutically applied be my guide as to which practices are sinful and can open the door to demonic influence. However, I also let scripture and the interpretive tradition of the church be my guide as to determine the normative way the practice of sin is to be combatted and addressed that is through the atonement for sin that Christ accomplished on the cross. Clearly, scripture calls persons to repent of their sin and put their faith in Christ for forgiveness and deliverance from sin. Salvation was provided through Christ's work on the cross where the power of sin and death was destroyed. The way of the cross (*via crucis*) is the normative means by which persons are delivered from sin and Satan not a deliverance session.

However, there are times one may be bound too intensely by sin due to practice that is generational, intense, frequent, and over an extensive duration of time (thus my four variables that make up the bondage quotient in the assessment instrument) and may need intercession and help from the body of Christ through prayer, fasting, and deliverance. Also, there are occasions that one may be assaulted and afflicted by the devil that are not related to sin committed. One may be sinned against as in abuse or trauma, or one may be oppressed by the devil in an area of sickness, such as the epileptic in the gospels. Sin committed was not the problem, and hence repentance not the solution. One may need to confront the powers of darkness that are responsible for the affliction. Thus, the way of the cross may be the normative means to deal with sin and the devil, but there are situations that call for an authoritative confrontation in the name of Jesus with the evil one.

Yet again, some spiritual problems are neither sin nor demonic nor solely sin and/or the demonic but may involve other mental and emotional afflictions that vex the individual. These afflictions, though they may even implicate and involve spiritual factors, mainly call for the attention of a mental health care professional. The minister then is in need of resources that will help refer the person to one who can discern the etiology, diagnosis, nature, and treatment of the problem. Referral to such professionals is the best course of action rather than relying on one's own lack of expertise. Nevertheless, the minister can incorporate treatment from other professionals into an overall strategy of healing that will also involve the spiritual resources of faith, prayer, scripture, spiritual authority, and other operations of the Holy Spirit along with those of the medical profession to bear on the treatment and healing of the person.

Yes, this book was written for Christian deliverance ministers. It was also written for the believer in Christ who seeks victory over sin and Satan by the power and authority of Jesus Christ but who also need to realize that not all spiritual problems are due to sin and/or the demonic and solved by deliverance. Some problems are best addressed in partnership with medical and mental health related professionals. However, this book was also written for the scientifically minded and the health care professional whose training rules out a spirit worldview and the existence of invisible causes like evil spirits that inflict the soul and body of the distressed. Those that dismiss such phenomena as pre-scientific and pre-critical may be surprised to find that the world of science enveloped by quantum on the micro end and dark energy and matter on the macro end is riddled with uncertainty and indeterminacy. Further, compiled parapsychological and religious cases and experiences that transcend the explanatory scope and power of the sciences are providing alternative frameworks and explanations that contest scientific reductionism.[2] Although these explanations may be discounted by some in the scientific community, they have a rational basis for belief and may provide a more satisfactory accountable narrative than what science has reduced or explained away.

Hundreds of first hand, scientifically inexplicable encounters by the author in deliverance ministry of visual or auditory (apparitions, demons, voices and shrieks while no one present), involuntary (twitches and jerks), supernatural (felt presences, levitation of bodies, inhuman strength, moving and throwing of objects without a visible presence to account for the action), and paranormal (multiple personalities, changes in voice, giving of random or odd historical accounts from voices that claims to be

2. Note, Craig Keener, *Miracles: The Credibility of the New Testament Accounts, two vols.* (Grand Rapids: Baker, 2011) and Randy Clark, *Eyewitness to Miracles: Watching the Gospel Come to Life* (Nashville: Thomas Nelson, 2018) as key texts that cite numerous cases of the supernatural work of God over against causal closure.

from other times and places) manifestations as well as testimonies of deliverance and relief from these manifestations attest to the same reality that Jesus ministered to in first century Palestine as recorded in the gospels. Of course, the experiences of the author are not anomalies or isolated but are also the experience of many ministers who practice deliverance and exorcism.

The premise in this wholistic strategy is that there truly is a place for integration between faith and the sciences, and that such integration is a more compassionate and effective strategy for healing and wholeness than one that does not involve integration but relegates the treatment to merely scientific means without the Spirit or relegates treatment to faith without God's gifts of medicine, therapy, and natural practices and remedies (i.e. sleep, diet, exercise etc.). Wisdom uses all of the healing gifts of God in the storehouse, old and new, natural and supernatural. This work is an attempt to assist in that very divine and very natural process of healing.

Acknowledgments

I WANT TO THANK both Dr. Mark Chironna and Dr. Randy Clark for their inspiring ministries and seasoned wisdom. I draw from their wells as often as possible. I am forever grateful for the Foreword to which they both contributed kind and insightful words that capture well the balance and intent of this work. I also wish to thank some of the churches that I have pastored over the years for offering me the opportunity to serve in ministry, including Faith United Methodist Church, Higher Ground United Methodist Church, Otterbein United Methodist Church, New Hope United Methodist Church, Ohmer Park United Methodist Church, and Westville United Methodist Church. I wish to thank United Theological Seminary, my colleagues, and students for granting me the opportunity to share the gift that God has given to me. I especially want to thank Matthew Johnson and Erin McKenzie for editing the document and making needed suggestions. I thank my wife Mariuccia and my children Pietro Aaronne and Paola Arianna for filling my heart and life with purpose. Above all, I wish to thank the Lord Jesus Christ who conquered my life with his love and the Holy Spirit for teaching me how to minister healing to the broken hearted.

1

Introduction

> "For he has rescued us from the dominion of darkness and brought us into the kingdom of the Son he loves."
> Colossians 1:13 (NIV)

MY BAPTISM INTO DELIVERANCE MINISTRY

As I RECOUNTED IN the Preface, my unforeseen initiation into spiritual warfare and deliverance began as a campus open-air evangelist sharing the gospel amidst a firestorm of opposition from the occult community at the Ohio State University. Outdoor preaching was a longstanding tradition in that university setting with students eagerly cutting class and gathering at the Oval (OSU's version of a quad) to hear and heckle the outdated, awkward Bible-banging preachers. Following the first week of my conversion to Christ back in the 1980s, I felt the call to share the gospel with my fellow Buckeyes and set out for the Oval on a daily basis to preach the good news. Old time revivalistic, fire-baptized, Holy Ghost convicting preaching seemed to stir up the sleeping, sinister sprites at that time, or the mere oddity of daily outdoor preaching at a major secular university in the late twentieth century rubbed some the wrong way. Perhaps both. In any case, my colleague and

I found ourselves regularly accosted by a group of self-proclaimed witches and Satanists, two in particular, who claimed they were cursing our ministry and having black masses for our death.

In that season, we prayed more intensively in our devotional time, meticulously "put on the armor of God," and interceded with prayers of divine protection. Not disturbed by the rants and harangues of the naysayers, we continued our regular outdoor preaching schedule, but the harassment and threats likewise continued until a startling incident happened to my friend one night. He called me after the incident and related the following that went something like this:

> I was in my bed trying to fall asleep when I saw an apparition at the foot of my bed that scared the @#X* out of me. Those two crazy witches that have been praying curses against us appeared in my room. I am not kidding . . . I freaked out and began to pray . . . They disappeared . . . Then shortly after the phone rang. I answered it. I heard a female voice say, 'Did you see us?' and the voice began to laugh menacingly along with another cackling female voice in the background. I quickly hung up the phone.

Needless to say, I was a little shaken and taken aback as a fairly young believer. For a moment, I questioned the veracity of my colleague's story and thought maybe his imagination had gotten the best of him after hearing the frequent threats against our lives by those two self-proclaimed witches. Yet, in my spirit, I felt he was truly sharing what he had experienced. I began to pray for discernment as to what was our next move. They had already planned theirs. One Sunday we found them parked at our home church sitting in their car. Not long after, they were regularly attending services on Sundays and Wednesdays, especially evening services.

They managed to fit perfectly into our small non-denominational, charismatic church, playing the part well. It was as if they rehearsed this scene methodically. Almost like they had performed it before. They usually were clothed conservatively in dresses or long skirts. They clapped to the praise music. Lifted up holy hands when the music shifted from high praise to deep worship. They warmly shook everyone's hand and invitingly hugged every neck when the preacher told the congregation after the first praise song to "go and greet each other." During the sermon, the ominous pair would "amen" at the right moment and shout along with the best of them. During ministry time at the end of service at the altar, they would routinely come up front with hands lifted high ready to receive prayer and even a word from God. The whole charade was quite eerie, and something I had never witnessed before or ever since.

The congregation did not suspect anything. In fact, some of our friends in the church rebuked us when we refused to embrace the two visitors during the "greeting time." We were actually stand-offish and a little rude with our ghoulish guests because we knew the truth, as did they. Weeks went by, and they consistently arrived an hour early before every service, camped out in their blue Trans-Am. We assumed they came early to pray against the service, the pastor, and the people of the church. Their part was well rehearsed and their performance stellar, even award-winning . . . until the revivalist came to town.

It was that time of the year, and our church brought in an evangelist. We were holding revival for the next few weeks, as any Spirit-filled church would do in the summer. The evangelist was a powerful African-American woman preacher who was also a seasoned prophetess highly fluent in the gifts of the Spirit and dripping with spiritual authority. The sanctuary was packed that evening, especially with many new faces as is customary during revival season. Our stealth sorceresses blended in well, and the service went as usual with the same mocking routines repeated seamlessly. However, at the conclusion of her preaching, the prophetess began to operate in the word of knowledge and call people out who had various issues, again, as is customary in a Spirit-filled church under the direction of an anointed servant of God. However, this time was different for both the prophetess and our two friends.

Following the word of knowledge, both of these pernicious performers came forward with hands raised, the elder standing in front of her apprentice. Immediately, as the woman of God laid hands on the elder witch, the prophetess boldly exclaimed, "We have two witches in the house!" In that very second, the spellbound and startled woman hit the floor and began to scream. The prophetess followed her to the ground, rebuking the spirit of witchcraft, and commanding the slithering figure to repent from her practice and surrender to Christ. The angry woman still screaming, "No, no, my power!" would not yield. My friend and I were elated and energized, as we shot up out of our pews and ran to the altar behind the fallen witch, almost waiting for the prophetess to retrieve a bucket of water to pour on both of them in order to liquidate them, à la *The Wizard of Oz*. We were young and later repented for our misguided zeal. For us, the culmination of events leading to this Elijah-Prophets of Baal Smackdown was both an adrenaline blitz as well as a comic conclusion to what was developing initially into a drama and a tragedy.

After lying on the carpet for a few minutes, the elder witch, still screaming and writhing on the floor, managed to get to her wobbly feet, quickly grabbed the wrist of her whimpering apprentice, and made a mad dash for the door never to be seen again. Yes, that was the last we ever saw or heard of them. Praise God! We hoped and prayed, though, that one day those two precious souls would heed the call to repent of their dark arts and come to Christ for deliverance and restoration. This was my glorious baptism into the deliverance ministry.

ON THE NAME OF THE INSTRUMENT

The demonic is real. However, the ministry of casting out demons is either entirely dismissed on the one hand or misused and abused on the other. A strict ratio-empirical, closed-system, natural, worldview utterly rejects the notion of a spirit world with spirit beings. To the other extreme, some inept and careless deliverance ministries reject the validity of the health professions and identify every problem in the life of the believer as demonic. The theology of these ministries fails to account for the power of the cross and its daily application in the life of the believer as the normative way in which God delivers from sin and evil. All challenges in the life of the believer do not necessitate a deliverance session. A balanced perspective on these matters including an instrument that can be used to assist in discerning the probable need for deliverance is essential. The creation of this integrative instrument comes out of my field experience in ministry with those afflicted by the demonic, mental disorders, and other ailments. Simply put, I learned that not one method works for all cases. I specifically realized this when applying deliverance to those struggling with mental disorders, such as bipolarity and schizophrenia. Merely casting out demons did not bring either immediate or long-term results. If I wanted real, transformative results, I needed to change my methodology. At that point I began to develop an integrative approach with a wholistic methodology that is reflected in this instrument.

The C1-13 is a qualitative and quantitative probability indicator for deliverance. The C1-13 instrument was developed to assist persons in discerning the probable need for deliverance in any given case. This assessment employs an extensive inventory to identify sinful practices and accompanied symptomatology to ascertain the probability of demonic involvement. The C1-13 then assigns values to four variables related to each sinful practice that are evaluated to determine an overall BQ—Bondage Quotient. The BQ is a score that is evaluated to determine if there is a need for deliverance.

This instrument has been given the lengthy title *The C1-13 Integrative Deliverance Needs Assessment* to describe the multiple functions of this tool. Due to the length and word choice of the name of the instrument, a brief explanation is warranted for the reader. As a professor, minister, deliverance practitioner, and a researcher, I designed this instrument as a way for individuals and deliverance teams to discern with more clarity and certainty the need for deliverance. The intention is to not rush impulsively into casting out demons uninformed. This instrument is also an attempt to move beyond simple checklist inventories of certain practices to indicate a measurable need for intercessory deliverance. Simple inventories and descriptions of sinful practices are what are commonly found in most books and resources on the subject. They are helpful but are often not in conversation with the findings and work of other professional fields, nor do they attempt to measure degrees of demonic influence and bondage. Degrees of demonization indicate that not all demonized persons are possessed, which is actually a rare state. Demons can have a varying degree of influence in a person's life.

In addition, some cases that may be erroneously labeled demonic may be primarily related to a mental disorder. In many cases, such inventories and popular books on deliverance do not distinguish the difference between mental disorders and the demonic, nor do they consider collaborating with other professional fields as beneficial to the overall efficacy of their work. In terms of mental disorders, the premise of some of these works is that God works through deliverance but not through therapy or medication. However, when the work of the health professions is disregarded, the result can be malpractice, misdiagnosis, improper treatment, and even exacerbation of the problem. In the worst case, suicide can be the result. This instrument presupposes the necessity for collaboration to arrive at a more comprehensive and wholistic picture and approach to the problem. In doing so, the tool seeks maximum results in wholistic treatment.

Additionally, in terms of popular inventories, they do not calculate variance in sinful practice and thus the *probable* need for deliverance. Not all sin, or sinful practice, is the same in terms of the need for deliverance. If deliverance is needed, the manner in which deliverance is carried out varies as well, based on the type of practice and degree of demonization. With many of the current deliverance models, all sinful practice is considered the same regardless of type, number of generations that have practiced, frequency, duration, and intensity of the practice. This research, which is also based on field experience, has developed four variables that account for such variation that make up a Bondage

Quotient that is used as a composite score to measure the probable need for deliverance. The four variables for measuring sinful practice are generational sin, frequency, duration, and intensity. Thus, multiple factors make up the assessment to determine the need for deliverance and not one single factor.

The term "C1-13" in the title is taken from Colossians 1:13, "He has delivered us from the domain of darkness and transferred us to the kingdom of his beloved Son." Jesus' finished work on the cross is the efficient cause, basis, and authority for deliverance. Christ has delivered us from the power of darkness and has transported us into God's kingdom. Christ is a deliverer, and the work of salvation involves deliverance. Deliverance is from the power of evil, sin, and death and therefore is a vital aspect of regeneration and sanctification. Because our deliverance is from darkness to light and from one rule of authority to another, the operation needs to be thorough, decisive, systematic, and total. The work of salvation leaves no aspect of our lives untouched, as we transition from darkness to light. Such a thorough work warrants the need for an instrument that can assist in the detailed and meticulous nature of deliverance. The C1-13 intentionally cross-references other health fields and utilizes a multi-variable approach that can initiate the process of covering the complex terrain of deliverance. The cross-referencing of other health fields leads to the following term "integrative."

"Integrative" is used to indicate that the instrument works with other professional fields, such as general medical practice, psychiatry, clinical therapy, recovery, social work, sociology and anthropology of religions (for examining non-Christian belief systems), pastoral ministry, and other health-related and spiritual disciplines. The instrument refers and directs to other fields to attain a comprehensive picture and approach to wholeness. The operable theological anthropology is that we are not reduced to merely one compositional category of spirit, mind, or matter, nor are we the sum of all of these categories. As humans we are more than any one of these designations and more than the sum of these designations. We are made in the image of God (*imago Dei*), an integrated whole that reflects the purpose of the Creator that is to know, love, serve, and give glory to God.

As multifaceted beings living in a complex world, we resist any facile attempts at reducing the nature of humanity and its problems. Hence, every problem is not a demon, but also every problem cannot be reduced to being merely psychological, chemical, or material. Not only is evil a complex problem, but understanding the nature of humanity is also a complex problem. The best in theological anthropology generically identifies humanity as created in the image of God (*imago Dei*), a term that has been defined and unpacked in a multitude of ways. For example, the human person can be arguably construed in Scripture as a monism (a whole), a dichotomy (material and immaterial, body and soul, or body and spirit), or a trichotomy (body, soul, and spirit). Augustine viewed humanity as a union of soul and body, yet fallen due to Adamic sin. Boethius and Aquinas understood humanity as basically a rational creature. With Thomas the rational soul is made up of the will and the passive and active intellect. As opposed to the intellectualism of Aquinas, the voluntarism of Scotus and Ockham focused on the will, both divine and human (freedom). While on the other hand, Luther denied any natural freedom of the will. Later, Schleiermacher would put an emphasis on the human capacity of feeling over rationality. Postmodern attempts would locate human being in relationality. The point made here is not to catalog the entire scope of views in theological anthropology but to offer a sampling that demonstrates the complexity of the matter.[1]

Theologically across the board, most voices within the great tradition of Christianity recognize that there was a fall, and that it severely impacted all of humanity, though there are different views on how deep and how wide. Nevertheless, sin is complex and systemic and has its roots in all aspects of human life, and therefore the manifold consequences of sin are spiritual, mental, emotional, physical, and beyond. Thus an approach to healing and wholeness

---

1. Schultz, *Reforming Theological Anthropology.* Surveys and critiques the landscape of theological anthropology and offers an anthropology of relationality as a response to problems with classical constructs.

needs to address the entirety of what it means to be human. The integration of the human person entails that any aspect of our being (spiritual, intellectual, emotional, physical) bears and influences the others. For instance, what we do with our body, i.e. get restful sleep or intense exercise, impacts our mind that impacts our emotions and even our spiritual well being. The human person needs to be considered as a whole when addressing healing, health, and wellness.

The problem requires that we garner the best resources from faith and reason and from the Spirit and science to minister effectively in deliverance. Through God's prevenient grace both the gift of medicine and the gift of supernatural healing come from the Lord who causes the sun to shine and the rain to fall on the just and the unjust. These gifts are God's blessing to all people because God is good and desires to heal. The C1-13 integrates the work of the health profession with the wisdom of God's Word into a qualitative and quantitative assessment of practices to ascertain the need for deliverance.

Finally, "Deliverance Needs Assessment" is what the instrument seeks to determine or measure. Is there a need for deliverance? Identifying the need for deliverance may be more of an art than a science. The same is often said about diagnosing and treating mental disorders. With mental disorders, such as depression, etiology is ultimately unknown. Depression is not a physical entity or phenomenon but more of a multifaceted and multivalent condition, though there is a chemical component involved. Thus, we cannot objectively test, scan, or biopsy for depression like we can for diabetes, heart disease, or cancer. There is no full proof method or assessment for diagnosing depression. From the DSM- 5, a percentage of subjectively reported symptoms is employed to make the diagnosis (five out of nine symptoms, 55.5 percent). We know factors that contribute to depression, such as genetics, biochemistry, environment, trauma, abuse, stress, substance abuse, major life events, and other factors may be involved, but ultimately the cause is unknown. Our human frame is feeble, dwelling in a fallen world and is subject to stress, life wear and tear, corruption, sin, and even the demonic. Assessing the need for deliverance, though not nearly as empirical and verifiable (loosely at that) as diagnosing a mental disorder, is similarly an imprecise procedure due to the same unknown factors. However, like diagnosing depression, assessing the need for deliverance is related to identifying certain practices and accompanying symptomology.

The tool assesses the need for deliverance qualitatively by identifying sinful practices that may be linked to demonic activity and quantitatively by scoring those practices using four variables to arrive at a composite score that is evaluated in terms of a probable need for deliverance. Although the C_{1-13} is an instrument that uses qualitative data that has been assigned a quantitative value, it is an imperfect tool that points to the probable need for deliverance. In ascertaining the need for deliverance, there is an attempt to detect *a posteriori* (reasoning after the fact from sense experience) the invisible (the demonic) through the visible (sinful practices). From a purely scientific standpoint, detecting or proving the invisible in itself almost begs the question. Thus, a purely scientific instrument that detects entities that are not detectable by the five senses or by any other known instrument is not possible at this point. We can only work from the visible world of sinful practices back to the invisible world of the tempter with the guidance of the Word of God, the indwelling Holy Spirit, and the gifts of the healing professions to infer the influence of the demonic and the need for deliverance.

Although there is not a purely scientific instrument available for deliverance, it does not entail that ministers cannot be effective in their work. Deliverance is not a purely scientific process. Deliverance is primarily a spiritual process. Our chief instruments of discernment are the Word of God and the Holy Spirit. Both the Word of God and the Holy Spirit together function as our source of truth in deliverance ministry. The Word and the Spirit impart discernment to our hearts, as we seek the holiness of God and seek to liberate persons from the work of the devil. God's truth (the Word and the Spirit) is a lamp unto our feet and a light unto our path that leads to liberty.

The experience of those seasoned in deliverance ministry, as well as my own experience, confirms the essential work of the Holy Spirit in discerning demonic strongholds and strategizing tactics for liberation. The inward witness of the Spirit seems to offer an incorrigible, tautological, self-evident testimony to our spirit when the Spirit speaks truth. Yet, we are fallible. We make mistakes. We sin. Our hearing ear may not be as accurate as we imagined, or our heart may not be as pure as we perceived. We may be hearing the voice of self rather than God. Our sin may be blocking out the voice of the Spirit, preventing us from hearing God. In all of these cases, we are then obligated to discern and test the spirits concerning what we hear and sense. We test by the Word of God, by the fruit of the Spirit, by discernment in the body of Christ, and by the life lived of the one seeking deliverance. The C1-13 is a supplement to such a discerning process

The layout of this book leading to the assessment in chapter seven is as follows. Chapters two and three function as an apologetic for deliverance. Chapter two touches on a spirit worldview and considers the possibility of invisible phenomena and spirit causation from a scientific standpoint. Proof is neither required nor offered for such a worldview or the existence of spirit beings as a basic belief. However, the rationality of the invisible is briefly entertained, opening the door for future discovery and conversation in the sciences, rather than *prima facie* dismissal. Chapter three is an apologetic as to why deliverance is needed in the Christian life. Chapter four couches deliverance in a larger soteriology and theology of healing. Deliverance as an extraordinary intercessory ministry is distinguished from the normative means of deliverance that is personally resisting sin and the devil and walking the crucified life (*via crucis*). In chapter five, an integrative approach to healing and wholeness is considered, gathering the best resources available from faith and science. Chapter six explains the nature and function of the instrument itself and each of its components. Chapter seven is the C1-13 instrument. An example of a legal waiver of liability for a deliverance session is included in chapter eight. In chapter nine, basic practical guidelines for pre and post deliverance as well as the deliverance process itself are enumerated. Following deliverance, it is important to affirm the faith. The Nicene Creed is included in the Addendum, as well as some fundamental, scriptural faith affirmations regarding the believer's identity and life in Christ.

2

On Worldview

"For in him all things were created: things in heaven and on earth, visible and invisible . . ." — Colossians 1:16 (NIV)

THE DELIVERANCE ASSESSMENT INSTRUMENT in this work, like Scripture, assumes the existence of an invisible creation, a spirit world that is inhabited by spirit beings both angelic and demonic. Colossians 1:16 declares, "For in him all things were created: things in heaven and on earth, visible and invisible[1], whether thrones or powers or rulers or authorities; all things have been created through him and for him." Scripture seems to tacitly accept that creation is both visible and invisible. There is a world accessible to the five senses and an invisible world not accessible to the five senses but to faith. When we acknowledge creation in holy writ, we hold a worldview that encompasses both material and spiritual realities working together. Scripture is filled with accounts of divine agency working in both the invisible and visible worlds, as well as invisible beings such as angels and demons working in the visible world. On the other hand, we see visible beings, such as women and men, interacting through prayer and worship in the invisible realm, as their prayers are lifted to heaven.

1. Kraft, *Christianity With Power.* A thorough treatment of a spirit worldview.

The traffic of agency flows both ways. There is divine-human interaction in the invisible and visible realms. The created world is both invisible and visible, and the two aspects of the created world are interconnected. For example, what is often called "Jacob's ladder" (Gen 28:12-13 and John 1:51) resembles a staircase between the invisible and visible worlds that depicts angels descending and ascending from heaven to earth. Angels are ministering the will of God in the world, while demons are seeking to thwart it. Scripture is replete with exchange between the invisible and visible realms.[2] We note this clearly in the life of Jesus who talks to his heavenly Father, is filled with the Spirit beyond measure, is ministered to by angels, heals the sick, works miracles, raises the dead, and casts out demons. Jesus interacted with spirit beings in the heavens and earthly beings in this world. Christ's worldview encompassed both the visible and the invisible, even the demonic. In fact, Jesus was among many things, an exorcist.

Simply, Jesus cast out demons and commanded his disciples to do likewise. Is Jesus operating merely out of a premodern or precritical worldview so that what he is addressing is merely hermeneutical (his interpretation) rather than ontological (real beings)? Is Jesus either wrong or limited in his interpretation of worldview? Stated another way, is Jesus ministering to the afflicted with both healing and exorcism, because the ailments and treatment are interpreted through a premodern worldview and standards? And if Jesus came today with our post-Enlightenment worldview, he would not cast out demons and lay hands on the sick but would refer persons to medical professionals? Usually the demonic encounters of the gospels are demythologized or explained in scientific terms as mental disorders or physical illness.[3] Meaning that in light of modern science, we are more enlightened

2. Scripture itself presupposes such activity. See the book of Revelation as a salient example of supernatural activity (divine, angelic and demonic) working within the world.

3. As referenced throughout this work, the author does not hold to the notion that mental disorders are demons or ultimately caused by demonic activity, though the demonic can seize the opportunity of mental disorder to wreak further havoc.

and are aware of the exact physical nature of these first century afflictions and need not resort to demonology. However, this line of thinking is problematic and is clearly not the case. Today, we are not aware of the exact physical causes of mental disorders, nor do modern treatments offer a cure but relief and improvement. Similarly, there are many physical diseases that remain incurable. Likewise, sin that opens the door to the demonic is not outdated and is as prevalent and profuse as ever.

Once again in terms of mental disorders specifically, medical science does not know the ultimate origin or cure of mental disorders either, and clearly cannot reduce such disorders to physical illness or some physical properties, even with our modern materialist worldview. Mental disorders are not simply physical and identifiable diseases, though they have neural chemical aspects, as well as many other aspects or components that are genetic, biological, environmental, psychological, and social. The physical or biomedical model cannot fully explain mental disorder and thus is not 100 percent precise on etiology or treatment. Nor does the biomedical model understand and cure all non-mental (physical) disorders and ailments either. The question remains does our modern post-Enlightenment worldview with the advances of medical science understand what Jesus and his disciples were facing in ministry any more than persons in the first century Greco-Roman world? Perhaps in some sense but not exhaustively. There is still the problem of "spirit." Remaining modern intangibles and uncertainties related to etiology, cure, sin, and the problem of evil are comprehended by Scripture in terms of broader concerns related to "spirit" or spiritual issues, such as a spirit worldview, spirit beings, and God as Spirit. Holy writ understands the problem of evil and its collateral damage in the world in terms of demonic agency, the universal fall, human freedom and sin, and redemption in Christ.

Scripture does not have a problem with a spirit worldview, spirit beings, divine and angelic action, or deliverance from demonic powers and neither does the great tradition of the church. In regards to demonic powers and deliverance, throughout the apostolic,[4] pre-Nicene and post-Nicene ages,[5] the church has acknowledged the existence of demons and practiced deliverance and exorcism through its rites. The medieval church as a rule ministered exorcism rites, illustrated most notably with St. Francis of Assisi.[6] Spiritual warfare against evil spirits was also a standard feature of Puritan sanctification.[7] The scientific revolution and the deism of the Enlightenment period challenged the notion of interaction between the supernatural and natural realms. However, revivalists during the age of reason, such as John Wesley, regularly encountered and battled the demonic.[8] Although the post-Enlightenment church has at times wrestled with the notion of the demonic and the validity of deliverance, it has still practiced deliverance throughout the Global East and South and even in the West.[9] Deliverance and exorcism continue to be *charisms* exercised in the modern church as well, while the Roman Catholic and Eastern Orthodox Churches have practiced their exorcism rites unbroken since their incipience.[10] Along with the witness of the major Christian traditions, I call upon the numerous testimonies of my vast array of colleagues[11] who have ministered in deliverance for decades that account for the existence of the demonic. My own deliverance ministry that includes thirty years experience

4. Twelftree, *In the Name of Jesus.*

5. Dauton-Fear, *Healing in the Early Church.*

6. Forcen, "St. Francis of Assisi," and Forcen and Forcen, "Demonic Possessions and Mental Illness," 258–79.

7. See Gurnall, *Christian in Complete Armor.*

8. See Webster, *Methodism and the Miraculous* and Daniel R. Jennings, *The Supernatural Occurrences.*

9. Alexander, *Signs and Wonders,* and Knut, *Pentecostalism and Witchcraft.*

10. Collins, *Exorcism and Deliverance Ministry.*

11. See the work of Mark Chironna, founder of Church on the Living Edge and Global Awakening under founder, overseer, and work of revivalist Randy Clark who is ministering healing and deliverance on every continent in the world through notable missionaries like Heidi and Rolland Baker in Mozambique. They have seen healing and deliverance of all types, even raising persons from the dead. Also see Clark, *Eyewitnesses to Miracles* and *Biblical Guidebook to Deliverance.*

on four continents with countless cases of demonic encounters and deliverances involving every imaginable situation in the seven categories of this assessment (chapter 7), including the occult, namely Satanism and black magic, testifies of the stark reality of the demonic. Many of these encounters yielded explanations and deliverances that a purely scientific worldview with its medicine, psychology, and sociology failed to generate.

Of course, the notion of a spirit worldview, spirit beings, and invisibility in general are still heavily contested and often held in contempt by sizeable segments of the mainline Christian church and our modern world that are vastly informed by science and a ratio-empirical (reason and senses) worldview. In our scientific worldview, if we cannot perceive something with our five senses, then we cannot understand it with our reason, and thus we dismiss such things as not real. Accordingly, scientists often dismiss the existence of angels, demons, heaven, hell, miracles, and even the existence of God. Though, we cannot prove according to the hefty, modern burden of the word "prove"[12] with incorrigible ratio-empirical certainty that an invisible realm exists, we are making a claim that a Spirit world does indeed exist and hold this claim to be a basic belief that is also rational. The contention is that perhaps scientism has exorcized demons from its worldview, but it has not exorcized them from the world. Only the Spirit can do that. We will briefly examine the plausibility and rationality of this basic belief.

INVISIBILITY, SCIENCE AND UNCERTAINTY

The problem, *prima facie,* for many in a visually oriented world may be the invisible nature of a posited spirit world. Simply, we are being asked to believe in the existence of things, we cannot see or

---

12. The modern epistemological crisis initiated by Descartes requires that if we cannot know everything beyond any doubt, then we can know nothing at all. Very little epistemologically has been able to sustain this foundationalist type of modern burden of proof that can be unnecessarily too heavy for any proposition or system, including science, to bear.

perceive, which goes counter to our senses. 'Seeing is believing' is our operating principle. Nevertheless, in terms of invisibility, the phenomenon of visibility is limited to a narrow window of visible light (human ocular sensitive) on the vast electromagnetic spectrum. The majority of the energy on the electromagnetic spectrum is not visible to our senses. Furthermore, 90 to 95 percent of the entire universe is made up of dark energy and dark matter that are not responsive to light.[13] In this sense, most of the universe is invisible rather than visible.

Of course, this fact does not prove the existence of a spirit world or angels and demons, though proof is not the intention rather plausibility. However, the proverbial 'there is more to reality than meets the eye' is not out of the question. Visibility may be related more to detectability. Perhaps the invisible is undetectable because the proper instrument has not been made available or is not being employed. What if what is needed is the proper instrument suitable to the object in order to perceive it? For example, John Wesley understood faith as a sixth sense suited to perceive the invisible. Perhaps, only spirit can perceive spirit, as 1 Corinthians 2:14 declares, "The person without the Spirit does not accept the things that come from the Spirit of God but considers them foolishness, and cannot understand them because they are discerned only through the Spirit."

Our certainty about what is or is not may not always have full proof. There is mystery in the universe that transcends our perception and understanding and may only be discernible by extraordinary means. Phenomena can exist like dark energy and not be detectable by ordinary ocular means. This first argument is more of a common sense objection to 'seeing is believing.' The second obstacle to a spirit worldview is more of a scientific hurdle, and it deals with causality. Many astrophysicists and other scientists hold the notion that the universe is causally closed (causal closure) and that physical laws of the universe are sufficient to explain all of the entities, systems, dynamics, and events in the universe. Basically, the universe is entirely physical, and all physical states have

13. See Panek, *Four Percent Universe*.

physical causes that are identifiable.[14] The implications are clear. There can be no spiritual causes, divine, angelic, or demonic, and hence no spiritual causal activity imposed on physical states. The causal closure claim is strict and unyielding towards claims of the supernatural. However, causal closure is also debated at various levels. Some out of an emergence framework[15] claim that causality may be open at the quantum level for upward causation and/or open at the level of consciousness for downward causation.

Emergence is an interdisciplinary framework that attempts to explain the activity and interaction of systems, properties, and actions within and between the various levels of fields that comprise the study of the universe from the microphysical upward to the macrophysical, meaning the quantum physical to the chemical, biological, psychological, sociological, and onward. The attraction to emergence is its explanatory power and that it eludes the extremes of reduction on one end and dualism on the other. Although emergence distinguishes that the universe is physical and involves many systems and supervenient properties (even immaterial ones like consciousness), it captures the relationship between levels of phenomena without reducing any level to the level below it, i.e. to say that all mental activity is merely and solely brain chemistry (reductionistic physicalism), [16]or that because one states that

---

14. Kim, *Supervenience and Mind*, 280.

15. The IEP states, "we could say that a property is emergent if it is a novel property of a system or an entity that arises when that system or entity has reached a certain level of complexity and that, even though it exists only insofar as the system or entity exists, it is distinct from the properties of the parts of the system from which it emerges." *Internet Encyclopedia of Philosophy: A Peer-Reviewed Academic Resource.* https://www.iep.utm.edu/emergenc/, *Stanford Encyclopedia of Philosophy* claims that "a property is said to be emergent if it is a new outcome of some other properties of the system and their interaction, while it is itself different from them. O'Connor and Hong, "Emergent Properties." https://plato.stanford.edu/archives/sum2015/entries/properties-emergent/. For an example of a scientific and theological explanation of the possibility of interactionist property dualism between consciousness and spirit agency and downward causation, see Clayton, *Adventures in the* Spirit, 128.

16. Kim, "Metaphysics of Reduction," 726–48.

all mental activity is merely brain chemistry then mental activity truly does not exist (eliminative materialism).[17]

The possibility of open causality in quantum and consciousness will be briefly explored. The challenge of accepting some of the stringent assertions of a physicalist's universe verging on reductionism is that when we observe the universe more intensely, we discover an underlying indeterminate dynamic that could possibly allow for causation, perhaps upward and even downward that is outside of the accepted closed physical, natural order.

Quantum theory and quantum mechanics, which describe reality at the micro level that undergird and govern the entire universe from the lowest level up, also illustrate the uncertainty and unpredictability of the cosmos and our limited ability to fathom it. The enigmatic quantum world is inundated with paradox and perplexity that have an impact on the overall cosmos. For example, take light that is a fundamental phenomenon for the existence of life and serves as the limit for the speed of energy and information transmission in vacuum (according to special relativity). According to quantum theory, light behaves ambiguously as both particle and wave (wave-particle duality). The accepted Copenhagen notion[18] of quantum that observation (specifically measurement) controls quantum dynamics is counter-intuitive. With the

17. Churchland, "Eliminative Materialism and the Propositional Attitudes," 382–400.

18. Often held to be the majority or orthodox, though disputed and loose, interpretation of quantum mechanics as initially proposed by Niels Bohr and Werner Heisenberg in Copenhagen, Denmark during the late 1920s. The interpretation notes that quantum theory predicts the probabilities of properties (location and momentum) measured in a system that are contained in the wave function of the particle and are collapsed out of superposition and into an eigenstate of observation. However, measurements of location and momentum cannot transpire simultaneously for the measurement of one impacts the measurement of the other, leaving one measurement inconclusive as expressed in Heisenberg's Uncertainty Principle. The controversial component of the Copenhagen interpretation is that it claims that observation collapses the wave function and its counter-intuitive speculations on reality including the breakdown of causality. See the work of David Bohm and others following for counter arguments (hidden variable formulations) to the Copenhagen interpretation

standard interpretation, the wave function of energy (according to Schrodinger's wave equation) collapses when measured or perceived, and the superposition (possible quantum states) of a particle collapses in reality in one location only when observed. And when one measures a particle's momentum, it impacts the particle's position and vice versa, creating uncertainty about the particle's properties (Heisenberg's Uncertainty Principle). The more we know of a particle's momentum, the less we know of its position and vice versa. Quantum theory exemplifies the uncertainty, unpredictability, and mystery in the universe, specifically causality, and our limitations in understanding it. Proof and absolute scientific certainty fall apart under quantum scrutiny.[19] With the indeterminacy of causality and probabilistic quantum outcomes, can it be possible that something outside of the natural order works as an agent on the natural order through quantum dynamics? Many scientists and theologians hold a version of quantum theology that postulates that it may be possible, even quantum non-interventionist objective divine action.[20]

Quantum theory also demonstrates the mystery behind perceived phenomena and their tenuous connection with randomness and probability due to observation and quantum's limited impact due to decoherence. Ultimately, there is uncertainty and enigma behind the "why" of what we observe in the universe that may open a window outside of the cosmos to transcendent or supernatural agency and action. This belief can be basic and rational if demonstrated in quantum theory. Again, this does not prove the existence of a spirit world or angels and demons, but quantum, one of the most powerful and consistent, though cryptic, dynamics in the universe, does provide many exceptions to the rule. Science is not always definite. Observable reality remains a mystery in terms of causality and its ultimate nature. Exceptions to the rule make

19. For an uncomplicated introduction to quantum theory see McEnvoy and Zarate, *Introducing Quantum Theory*.

20. Polkinghorne, among others, believe that quantum (natural causal breakdown either due to uncertainty or entanglement) may be the missing link and causal hinge between the supernatural and natural realms. See Russell et al. *Quantum Mechanics*.

room for other possibilities and explanations, perhaps even a spirit world and spirit agency.

The scriptural notion of an invisible realm of spirit beings cannot be unequivocally ruled out. Certain interpretations of quantum theory show the plausibility and rationality of free agency acting on the physical universe. A biblical worldview that holds to a notion of spirit agency, which is held by majority world Christianity and other world religions, is reasonably plausible. As believers, we take scripture by faith and believe what it reveals about God, angels, demons, heaven, hell, miracles, the supernatural, and other invisible realities. The Bible calls us to believe in a God that we have never seen who saves us from a hell that we have never seen, and offers us eternal life in a heaven that we have never seen. Faith is an essential instrument of knowledge for the Christian. We believe in more than meets the eye. Reality is not just material or matter. We walk by faith and not by sight, like Moses *"who saw Him who is invisible"* (Heb. 11:27). Faith is the sixth sense that apprehends the invisible, which is perhaps what is required as pure physicalism is recently coming under harsh scrutiny.[21]

We lightly touched on the notion of open upward causation that may stem from some spirit agency upon the quantum field. Now let us briefly touch on the possibility of open and downward causation upon consciousness from a spirit agent and downward causation from consciousness interacting on the brain and other physical entities. Some of the current research in the philosophy of mind and related neurosciences postulates that there are properties of matter that cannot be reduced to matter itself but are intangible. Philosopher David Chalmers poses that consciousness is a property of matter that cannot be reduced to or explained by matter, though consciousness is supervenient on matter (property

21. Note that significant research has been done by scholars who have examined supernatural claims to healing and deliverance as responses to prayer. This research does not necessarily seek to find the causal joint between faith and science in order to create space in a scientific worldview for faith. Rather, it examines the claims (emic perspective) and evidence (etic perspective of medical science) itself for possible explanations and plausibility of causal connections. See, Brown, *Testing Prayer*.

dualism).[22] Chalmers recognizes that our unique experience of the material world cannot be reduced to the material world or cannot be explained solely by the material world. Our experience of blueness when we see the color blue or the beauty of a sunset is explained by the term *qualia*. The qualia of a thing are the way we experience or feel about particular perceptual or mental states that cannot be conveyed or explained by the physical data itself. Qualia are the subjective, perceived qualities of our experience of the external world. For example, the sensation of hearing the Beatles for the first time, or tasting a New York Strip Steak, or feeling vertigo when looking off the Brooklyn Bridge are all examples of qualia. And for each of us, the experience of these phenomena is qualitatively unique and thus different, even though physically and neurologically the laws of physics and neuroscience concerning the events are objectively the same for each of us.

Chalmers claims that qualia (a product of consciousness), and consciousness cannot be explained by physical reality. The inexplicability of consciousness is what he calls the "hard problem" of consciousness. Technically, one can have all of the physical reality or hardware that we have as humans like a "philosophical zombie" (the possibility of such a creature) or a machine needed to understand our world and not have consciousness or experience qualia. Think of a hungry customer seated in a restaurant who reads the entire menu of delectable entrees and asks the waiter all of the questions possible about each dish. That person can also exhaustively know all of the physiology, biology, and neurology at work when one eats. Further, the person can know all the details about every dish on the menu and the entire physics of eating but never have eaten and experienced one dish. Such a person cannot explain the phenomenal taste of the dish. Moreover, when one orders a particular dish like the beef enchiladas and deliberately enjoys every morsel, the scrumptious experience of that dish is not entailed in the knowledge of the menu or even explained by the enchiladas themselves. Knowing about the menu or even the

22. See Chalmers, *Conscious Mind*.

physics and neuroscience of eating does not entail experiencing the dishes on the menu.

There is a gap between the physical brain and the experience of the mind that cannot be explained by matter itself. The use of Chalmer's argument, which is just one of many for or against, illustrates the possibility that there is more to reality than the physical. The sum of what we experience is in excess and more than the parts that help produce it. Things like consciousness are intangible and cannot be explained by the physical world. What if consciousness were somehow related to spirit, and qualia were the experiences of the spirit world? There is a continuing emergence of theologians, philosophers, and scientists that posit the strong emergence of consciousness as a property of the brain but not reducible to it, and that consciousness can have some downward influence on lower level phenomena. For example, the psychological state of anxiety can downwardly influence brain activity creating different physiological states like high blood pressure, physical states like skin rashes, and even neural structural changes like neuroplasticity.[23] Furthermore, some would extend the properties of consciousness to include openness to the experience of spirit (divine, angelic, demonic) as qualia and even experience mutual interaction and influence from such qualia, opening the door to spirit agency and activity.[24]

Though this is just an experiment in thought and a cursory examination of spirit agency and activity, the point is that one can hold the notion that an invisible world with invisible beings may exist as a rational basic belief. The C1-13 instrument couples such a rational basic belief of spirit beings with the teaching of Scripture as interpreted by the church that such a world and such beings do in fact exist.

23. Clayton and Davies, *Re-emergence of Emergence.*

24. Clayton, *Adventures in the Spirit,* 14. Spirit reality is seen as an emergent property like consciousness.

3

Why Deliverance?

IN MATTHEW 10:7-8, WE find a summary of Christ's ministry and the ministry of the disciples, "As you go proclaim this message, 'The kingdom of Heaven has come near.' Heal the sick, raise the dead, cleanse the lepers, cast out demons. Freely you have received. Freely give."

Casting out demons and healing all of those who were oppressed of the devil were practices central to Christ's ministry. Deliverance ministry should be central to our ministry as well. Throughout the gospels, we find Jesus exercising authority over evil spirits and loosing persons who were bound and afflicted by the devil. In fact this aspect of Christ's ministry is so prominent that Jesus is often understood as an itinerant exorcist.[1] Jesus exercising the finger of God to cast out demons was a sign (*semeion*), one among many, that the kingdom of God has invaded and overthrown the kingdom of darkness (Luke 11:20). When the light breaks through, then the darkness flees, and people are set free from captivity. The release from evil oppression is a sign of the authority of the kingdom of God. In his name, Christ has given the same authority to us to overthrow darkness, cast out demons, and set prisoners free (Mark 3:27; 16:17; Lk 10:19). In the name of Jesus, we have the power and authority to bind and overthrow

---

1. See Twelftree, *Jesus the Exorcist*.

25

the "strong man" or ruling spirit of the house (soul or life of the person). Jesus set people free from demonic bondage and also commanded his disciples to do likewise.

As an inner city pastor, I remember a young man coming to my door seeking salvation in Christ. Our family lived next to the church in the parsonage. He and his brother were warlocks and necromancers. On the weekend, late at night, they frequently visited cemeteries and would sit on gravestones and summon the dead, conversing with spirits for prognostic information, ecstatic experiences, and spiritual power. Needless to say after some time, this man became brutally oppressed by demonic spirits. He had also indulged in a life of drug use, rampant sexual exploits, and criminal activity. By the time he came to the church where I was pastoring, he was a beaten man looking for freedom. As a youth, he had visited several churches and had heard of Christ and the salvation offered to all persons. That night he came to the parsonage to talk to me about his situation and his desire for freedom.

He shared his story with me, my wife, and our community minister for nearly two hours. He candidly revealed the entire sordid narrative of his life, focusing heavily on the last few years of indulging in witchcraft and drug use. After he had finished his story, which included an admission that his practices were not acceptable to God and a plea for liberation, I began to give him assurance that Christ could deliver him, if he was sincerely ready to give up these practices, open his heart to believe on Christ, and commit to a life of following him according to the scriptures. He agreed, and we prayed.

Needless to say, God showed up, but in a way that was unexpected by all of us, including our friend. I laid hands on the young man, and he fell to the ground. We knelt besides him and continued to pray. In that moment, something occurred that I have never encountered before in my ministry. The man began to levitate. His red eyes rolled back until all that we could see were the whites of his eyes. Light smoke came out of his eyes and mouth, as he began to growl and hiss in a voice that was not his own. Once again, he did all of this while levitating off of the ground around four to five inches off the floor! So much for scientific worldview and causal closure!

With one knee on the floor, I lifted my other leg and rested my knee onto his stomach, while I lightly pressed on his chest hoping he would slowly descend and rest on the ground. It did not happen. I increased both weight and pressure from the knee and from my palms, as I attempted to press him to the ground while we continued to war in the Spirit against these demonic forces. Currently, I am a five foot, ten inch, 250 lbs. recreational powerlifter and boxer who can bench press 405 lbs. At the time, I weighed a little less and pressed only around 320 lbs. Point being, I was no featherweight. This levitating young man held my weight and pressure while remaining suspended for what seemed around two or three minutes, until we prayed through in the Spirit and broke the stronghold at which time he descended to the ground. We continued to pray for the next few hours until the young man had peace and committed his life to Christ. We would work with him over the next several years helping him to full restoration and wholeness through discipleship and referrals to mental health professionals.

Demonic activity is real. In the prayer our Lord taught his disciples, he prayed "Lead us not into temptation, but deliver us from evil." Jesus knew we needed deliverance and taught us to pray for it. "To deliver" means to set free, release, rescue, or liberate. In the context of the Lord's Prayer, deliverance is from temptation (to sin) and evil. Jesus teaches us to pray to be released and liberated from the power of temptation and evil. Jesus prayed that we would be delivered when tempted to participate in the work of evil. God answers that prayer by giving us the power to resist the devil when he tempts us to sin. At times, when unbelievers or believers are bound in sin and cannot resist and free themselves, they need intercessors to pray and go to war on their behalf for deliverance from sin and evil. We can intercede for those bound in sin and pray deliverance on behalf of those in captivity. The need for this type of deliverance (intercession for deliverance) from sin and demonic influence arises when we fall into the practice of sin and even manifest traits of being bound by the devil. This instrument assesses the need for intercessory deliverance from sin. What is sin and evil? Anything that is against the nature and will of God as revealed in the Bible is sin and is the work of evil.

SIN IS LINKED WITH THE DEMONIC

Scripture (i.e. Gen. 3:1-5 and Rev. 12:9) has always been clear that Satan is the author of temptation. His purpose in tempting us is to lead us into sin. The work of the devil is the device behind all temptation and sin. Through the connection of temptation and sin, we understand how sin is linked with the demonic, the tempter. The two are connected. Sin is what connects us to the work of Satan, and so persistent sin often necessitates deliverance from the demonic. Through sin, as one yields to the will of the enemy, one is not only bound together more tightly with sin, but one is also bound more tightly with the devil and his works. Sin can open the door to the demonic that in turn creates the need for deliverance from the demonic because the enemy's influence and authority increase over generations, frequency, intensity, and duration. When one submits to sin, one is submitting to the influence of the devil. The devil is the tempter and is the voice and power behind temptation, while temptation is the seductive bait that lures one to sin. The means of temptation or bait to sin are "doors" that the devil uses and crouches behind, waiting to enter into the human soul when one opens the door to sin (Gen. 4:7). Through sin, Satan gains influence in people's lives. We need to be aware of such doors not to open them but to subdue and rule over the desire to open the door and sin.

While God is omnipotent, the devil's power is fallen and limited. In fact, the sole power of the devil is the power of deception. His words and his work are without substance and function as deceptive shadows. He cannot create but only distort and destroy through the fallen power of deception. He is the father and inventor of lies. He creates lies to seduce us into sin, so that we may be condemned to death. His mission is to deceive and to destroy. On the other hand, God reveals truth to set us free. The devil's lies bind us and bring us into bondage, but the truth of God's Word liberates and delivers. The key to deliverance and spiritual warfare is to discern between the lie of the enemy and the truth of the Word of God. At times, discerning the lie of the enemy can be difficult. Satan seduces persons with an alternative and false reality that he concocts with his deceptive words that function like incantations and sorcery on our thoughts and perceptions (Rev. 18:23). Through his witchcraft, he creates a false reality, telling us what God said will bring us death will really bring us fulfillment. The lie creates and crafts the binding power of temptation that captures the human will in sin. When the devil coaxes us to sin, he has deceived and entrapped us to do his will and thus has gained some degree of power and control over us in that area. Such bondage can occur not only with unbelievers but also with believers. If one has the capacity to sin, regardless if one is a believer or an unbeliever, one can be influenced by the devil. Believer and unbeliever alike can be bound in sin. Thus, believer and unbeliever alike may need deliverance from sin.

It is essential to know that the need for deliverance does not entail that one is possessed of the devil, which is actually a rare state. Demonization or demonic influence comes in degrees. The need for deliverance signifies that the devil has some degree of influence and control over one's will in a particular area(s). One may be walking in victory in most areas of the Christian life but still be deceived and bound in one particular area, such as anger, jealousy, or lust. Here, demonization means degree of demonic deception and influence over the will.

Consequently, anyone who is tempted and gives into sin has fallen into the work of the devil. The remedy is to resist sin, rebuke or cast out the devil, and yield one's will to God's will, which is deliverance. Deliverance means to be set free from sin and evil. Deliverance is a practice that, by the grace and power of God, we can freely execute when needed. Nonetheless, when the will is bound and demonization is too great to break free, intervention is needed. Intercessory deliverance is the act of liberation, performed by one or more believers that assists the one who is in bondage to be set free. Following, the prayer of deliverance in the name of Jesus is prayed on that person's behalf. The C1-13 is an aid for this type of intercessory deliverance carried out by one or more persons on behalf of another. So to clarify, deliverance in the general sense of the word can be performed by individuals on themselves in the power of the Spirit when they resist sin and the devil. Deliverance, in the more specialized sense of the word, and the topic of this book, is when individuals are bound to the degree that they cannot deliver themselves and intervention is necessary. Specialized or intercessory deliverance is then needed.

Vital wisdom. All sin does not necessarily lead to the need for others to assist in a "deliverance session" or intercessory deliverance. In most cases, a person can resist the temptation and cast the voice and power of temptation and deception out of his or her own mind and submit to God. James 4:7 sums up scriptural deliverance from evil—"*Submit to God and resist the devil*." This type of general deliverance is the lowest level of spiritual warfare and involves daily personal resistance to temptation and sin by saying "no" to the devil and the will of the flesh, and "yes" to God and the way of the cross, which is death to sin. When the practice and power of sin increase to the point that the unbeliever's or believer's will is broken and captured, and one can no longer defeat sin and the devil in that area, that person may consider help from the body of Christ. There is a variety of assistance that can be offered. One way to help is to have a believer(s) stand in the gap and fight as an intercessor on one's behalf in prayer and specialized deliverance.

Another point of discernment is that not all deliverance is due to sin that one commits. Sin committed against a person can open the door to demonic attack, even though the person did not sin. Saul's jealousy against David opened up the door to demonic attack in David's life. Many, who have been sinned against, for example in abusive and traumatic situations, may be attacked, tormented, and bound by the devil. In these cases, such persons did not commit a sin but were sinned against. Doors to the demonic not only include sins we commit but also sins committed against us. The devil uses tragic experiences like abuse and trauma and the emotional damage connected to such experiences as a doorway into one's life. These experiences that expose our vulnerability provide opportunities for the devil to further profit and take advantage of our tragedies. Case in point, our church was located in one of the largest sexually oriented business districts in the country. As a response, our church launched a Women's Center to minister to those trapped in the sex industry. Our Center became one of the leading ministries in the nation that reached out to those affected by that industry. Over time, we learned that most of these women were sexually abused in the household as children and were later tempted by the devil into a life of promiscuity, drug use, and even into a life in the sex industry or were sexually trafficked. Early childhood trauma opened the door to further demonic attack and bondage. Some need healing and deliverance not only because of their sins, but also because of sins committed against them.

THE C1-13 INSTRUMENT

The C1-13 instrument was developed to assist persons in discerning whether deliverance is needed in a particular case by utilizing multiple variables that identify demonization. Using an instrument to detect invisible phenomena, like the demonic, is not full proof or an exact science, as referenced above. To measure something that you cannot directly observe and gauge quantitatively is challenging. This instrument, working with the inward witness of the Spirit, identifies doors (of sin) that are forbidden in scripture and recognizes accompanied symptomatology to ascertain possible demonic involvement. The assessment then assigns values to four variables for each sinful practice to determine an overall "BQ—Bondage Quotient" that in turn informs the likelihood for the need of deliverance. Even though this instrument offers a checklist to survey potential doors of demonic entry and evaluates demonic practices and manifestations or symptoms, the instrument hardly provides a clear-cut formula to determine the need for deliverance. Reliance on the witness of the Spirit is imperative, as well as referring to professionals when needed. As a confirming tool that seeks to detect the invisible, the instrument works with probability. Spiritual realities and phenomena cannot be measured neatly with numerical metrics. The witness of the Spirit is direct and can give assurance, but an instrument such as this works with approximation and functions as confirmation to the witness of the Spirit.

At the beginning of the assessment is a section requiring personal information, such as biographical information and medical history. Medical and psychological assessments from other professions that may have a bearing on the current problem are important factors to be considered when determining the need for deliverance. For example, mental health conditions can create many problems and symptoms that may seem similar to demonic manifestations or may open the door to demonic attack. Note that mental disorders are not to be confused with the demonic,[2] though the latter can take advantage of the weakness and disorientation brought about by the former. In my ministry, I have observed deliverance ministers fail to liberate persons with major depression, only to observe the same persons relieved of the "demonic" symptoms through medication and counseling. The medication did not "cast out" the demon. The SSRI[3] relieved the depression symptoms. If there were demons profiting from the mental disorder, then treatment closed the door of opportunity by dealing with the depression itself. A mental disorder is not synonymous with a demon, though demons surely can work through them. Thus, some familiarity with relevant sections of the DSM-5 (Diagnostic and Statistical Manual of Mental Disorders), symptomatology, and recommendation of professional help when

2. Spiritual warfare experts like Ed Murphy, Paul Loren Sanford, and Neil Anderson recognize that mental disorders are not synonymous with mental demons and are not to be cast out but treated and healed. One way to overcome depression is to renew the mind with the Word of God. Depression itself may not be a demon to cast out, however, demons often co-work along side of mental disorders and take advantage of the opportunities that they provide. Treatment must be integrative.

3. Selective Serotonin Reuptake Inhibitor

needed, as well as supporting existing diagnoses and prescriptions can be vital. Proper psychiatric or other medical care, including unbroken pharmacological, dietary, or other treatment is essential prior to any clear assessment of demonic activity. True theology and true science should work together and are not in conflict. The Ten Point Checklist located in chapter seven helps to determine the need for professional referral. Professional treatment needs to precede taking the assessment. In this sense, a deliverance session is seen as a last resort.

4

A Brief Theology of Deliverance

"The reason the Son of God appeared was to destroy the devil's work."—1 John 3:8 (NIV)

IN THE BEGINNING GOD created the heavens and the earth, and they were good. God has blessed humanity with goodness and life and the power to choose to walk in God's blessings. In the garden, humanity was seduced to distrust God and to choose its own way. The insidious serpent instigated the way of rebellion against God and humanity succumbed. Through the power of deceit, the devil trapped and enslaved humanity to fulfill his mission to steal, kill and destroy. The good news is that while we were yet sinners and enemies of God, Christ loved us and died for us so that we may be delivered from sin and evil and once again experience freedom and God's blessings. Note that the basis and power for deliverance is in Christ's work on the cross (death, burial, and resurrection).

We experience deliverance and fullness of life when we yield by faith to the work of Christ on the cross. The cross for the believer signifies the death and burial of the old life and resurrection of the new life. Walking in the way of the cross (*via crucis*) is the scriptural and normative method of deliverance from temptation and sin.[1] We die to sin by yielding to the sin destroying work of

1. Other leading experts in healing and deliverance such as Sandford

the cross. We are then renewed spiritually day by day through the Word of God, as we learn that we are a new creation in Christ. We are transformed by renewing our mind (Rom. 12:2). As our heart changes, our practices change as we walk daily in the Spirit. The sins we committed prior, we commit no longer. We resist the devil, and he flees. This rhythm is the scriptural, normative way persons are delivered from the power of sin and Satan, and it is the normative way that believers stay free and do not become entangled again in the bondage of sin (Gal. 5:1). The way of the cross (*via crucis*) is the normative New Testament method for salvation and sanctification and not the deliverance session. Repentance and faith in Christ is the standard way unbelievers come to Christ. Taking up our cross daily and crucifying the flesh in the power of the Spirit is the standard way that believers resist sin and stay free in Christ.

However at times, as noted above, one may be overwhelmed in one's walk and may be assailed by temptation and sin on every side. One may become so deeply bound in sin that he/she needs to be loosed. Due to deep-seated past brokenness, the weary soul may find it difficult to resist and may fall under the attack of the devil and into the bondage of sin. Deliverance as intercession is likely needed at this point. As a communion of saints, we pray for each other and confess our brokenness and even our sins that we may be healed. The saints of God rally in prayer for deliverance on behalf of the one who is bound.

As reference above, a balanced approach distinctly recognizes that every encounter with sin does not entail the need to cast out a demon from someone. A sound theology of sanctification stresses that the normative method of deliverance is resisting temptation and sin through the power of the Spirit (Rom. 8:13; Col. 3:5). The Spirit leads us to resist sin and yield to the death and resurrection of Christ. When we are in Christ, we become a new creation. It is our new standing. However, we experience the new creation through the daily renewal of the Spirit (2 Cor. 4:16). As a new creation in

---

and Sandford, *Deliverance and Inner*, 62–3,109–10 recognize that repentance, faith, and walking the crucified life are normative in dealing with sin over against deliverance.

Christ, we are also called to know who we are in Christ by having our minds renewed with the Word of God. The truth sets us free from the lies that bind us (Jn. 8:31-32). When God renews our minds with the truth, then our beliefs change. When our beliefs change, then our hearts will change, and so our sinful practices will change. Dying to the old life, walking as a new creation, and renewing our minds with the Word comprise the normative way we find deliverance from sin and evil. Nevertheless, there are occasions in which a bound person needs intervention. In deliverance ministry, we pray and minister the power of the cross in Christ's name on behalf of the oppressed. We minister Christ's authority as intercessors on behalf of another to liberate the captive and lead that person into new life.

THE TRIUNE GOD AND LIFE

The nature of God is eternal life (Jn. 17:3). The Triune God is a life-giving God. In Genesis 1:1, God brought all life into being. In 1 John 1:1, the second person of the Trinity is called the "Word of Life." In Roman 8:2, the Holy Spirit is called the "Spirit of Life." In the Nicene Creed, the Spirit is described as "the Lord the Giver of Life." The Lord gives life and restores life. As Lord, the Spirit brings life and liberty to all who are oppressed (2 Cor. 3:17). In fact, Jesus of Nazareth in Luke 4:18-19 was anointed by the Holy Spirit to proclaim release for the prisoners and to set the oppressed free. In John 10:10, Jesus said he came to bring "abundant life." In John 11:25, Christ declared that he is "the resurrection and the life," and reiterates the same claim in John 14:6 as "the way, the truth, and the life." Scripture witnesses throughout to the life of the Triune God, and God's desire to impart new life to all of creation.

The Triune God exudes everlasting and fullness of life in three persons. The Father declares life through his Word and breathes life through the Spirit, as evidenced in creation (Psalm 33:6) and the new birth (John 3:5). Through original creation and the new creation, we are made partakers of the same divine life that is in God (2 Peter 1:4). In God there is fullness of life, life that is eternal, life that quenches human thirst, living water, which quenches our thirst for true life.

THE FALL AND THE LAW OF SIN AND DEATH

Although God gives abundant life freely to all of creation, we resist God's grace and love and turn from his goodness. We refuse to partake of the tree of life but instead indulge in the tree of the knowledge of good and evil. The pages of the annals of human history show how we eagerly have chosen to be our own gods and stubbornly obey our own wills. Satan has cunningly seduced the human race to do what is right in its own eyes. Proverbs 14:12 informs us that *"there is a way that appears right to human eyes, but in the end it leads to death."* Correspondingly, the first part of Romans 6:23 declares, *"that the wage of sin is death."* Sin enslaves us and leads us to death. Death is the "reward" for sin. In unison, sin and death act universally on each of us. In Romans 7, Paul vividly describes in detail how the will is bound and enslaved to sin no matter how much it desires to do good. To paraphrase, when one attempts to do good, one discovers that evil is present. The evil that one does not want to do, one finds oneself doing. Paul recognized the dynamic of how sin enslaves the will and prevents it from doing the right thing. In Romans 7:21 he identified it as a "law" at work within us that counteracts every good intention with an inward response of evil. In Romans 8:2, we note that the work of sin results in death, the "law of sin and death." The law of sin and death rules over humanity with an iron fist. No one escapes its unbreakable clutch.

Although sin and death act on human behavior with the consistency and power of a universal law, they do not act alone or deterministically. Our will cooperates. God is not to blame and neither is the devil for our sin. We are passionately involved in the act of sin. James 1:14-15 indicates that one is tempted because of his or her own lust, and when one gives into lust, it conceives, and it conceives sin. There are two factors that help to set in motion the law of sin and death, our temptable nature and the tempter.

The first is our temptable human nature and the agency we have to make choices. As humans, we have needs that when rightly ordered by God's will enable us to live a fruitful life of purpose and meaning. Our God-given capacity for passions is good, since passions were intentionally created to be subject to kingdom (of God) order. However, when passions are not subject to kingdom order, they become sinful and can lead us to destruction.

For instance, one of those God-given needs is for companionship. Scripture lays the guidelines for lifelong covenantal companionship within the context of marriage between a man and a woman. The needs and desires we have for companionship, attraction, reproduction, and intimacy are drives given to us by God. In their proper order and place, they are good and holy. However, outside of God's order, these pursuits become self-serving, divisive, self-destructive, and sinful. Pleasure and persons become objectified. The bond of love that holds each person faithful to the other may be easily broken when marriage is not held as a holy covenant from God. In addition, the birthing and raising of children without the resources of a stable family may also be detrimental to parenting. Nevertheless, even in a fallen world, marriage and family structures can also experience the same destructive patterns as those outside of marriage.

These concerns and others arise when companionship or any other God-given need or capacity is pursued outside of the purpose and order of God. God creates us in his image with agency and the choice to follow his way or our own way. This choice is God's gift given to us and must be strongly factored into any analysis of deliverance. We make grave choices of obedience or rebellion and life or death. We choose to open up the door to God's reign or the reign of sin and Satan. When Christ comes to deliver us out of the kingdom of darkness and into the kingdom of light, he liberates our will from the power of sin to choose to obey God's will.

The second factor or catalyst for the law of sin and death is the existence of the tempter, the devil, and his temptations to lure us away from God and into rebellion. The voice of temptation was present at creation and in the first choices made, as our original parents were seduced by the evil one to disobey God. Even our Lord, who was fully divine and also fully human, was tempted as he walked the earth, though he did not yield to temptation. On many occasions, Satan consistently tried to lure Christ away from the will of the Father while in the desert, throughout his ministry, in the garden of Gethsemane, and on the cross. However, where humanity failed, Christ succeeded. Jesus chose to obey the Father and overcame temptation by the power of the Holy Spirit. On the cross, he defeated sin, death, and the devil on our behalf, so we may be delivered and walk in victory. On the cross in John 19:30, Jesus declared, "It is finished." He meant the power of sin, death, and the devil is finished. At the cross, the power of evil is destroyed. The work of the cross is truly our basis for deliverance and victory.

THE WAY OF THE CROSS IS GOD'S WAY OF DELIVERANCE

The use of the term, "the cross" or the "work of the cross" in this context is shorthand for the death, burial, resurrection, and ascension of Jesus Christ and all that these events theologically entail and provide for humanity and the rest of creation. Christ's work on the cross is the means by which God has dealt with sin, death, Satan, and all evil. He took sin and death in his own body and destroyed its power, so that we may be free from its tyranny (Rom. 8:3). Deliverance begins and ends at the cross. Deliverance, primarily, is not our work or by our effort, though God allows us to participate in the ministry of deliverance based on his work. The basis, authority, and power for all deliverance, either general or specialized, stems from the cross. The cross is the objective ground for deliverance and victory, while the work of the Spirit is the subjective implementation and manifestation of deliverance and victory. The Spirit working from the objective ground of the cross applies the experience of deliverance and victory to our lives. The Spirit works on the basis and in unison with the cross. The work of the Holy Spirit is to convict us of sin, righteousness, and judgment and lead us to Christ, our deliverer from sin (Jn. 16:8). In leading us to Christ, the Holy Spirit leads us to the cross of Christ, where God has destroyed the power of sin and death. The Spirit reveals God's will in Christ to reconcile the world unto him. The Holy Spirit shines the light on the messianic identity and mission of Christ. Further, the Spirit reveals that Christ has been sent by the Father as the Lamb of God who takes away the sins of the world. He discloses that Jesus Christ is the way, the truth and the life that leads us home back to the Father. The Holy Spirit unveils that Christ is the resurrection and the life and all of the other glorious titles and offices claimed of him in Scripture.

When believers surrender to the work of the Spirit in faith, they are led to the cross to behold the Son of God/the Son of Man. The Word became flesh to embody all that is broken and out of order in this world. He takes our sin and suffering unto himself and has tasted death for everyone that those who die may live forevermore. Yet, Christ not only took our sins to the cross, but he also took the sinner to the cross, so that the old life may die. When the Spirit leads us to the cross, he leads us to join Christ on the cross. He leads us to be baptized into his death, burial, and resurrection that the old life may die and new life may spring forth into eternity (our identification with Christ - Rom. 6:1-7). Not only does the Spirit lead us to die with Christ on the cross when we first come to Jesus, but he also leads us to deny ourselves daily and take up our cross and to follow Christ. We are joined moment by moment to die a deeper death in order to rise moment by moment to a higher life in Christ. We are called to put to death the sinful practices of the flesh and put on the new person in Christ (Rom. 8:13; Eph. 4:24-26; Col. 3:5). Romans 6:5 indicates that "we have been united in his death." The verb is in the perfect tense, meaning completed action in the past with ongoing results. We died to sin, but the effect of that death has continuing results in our daily walk by "mortifying the flesh" and "walking in the Spirit." The pattern of death and resurrection is a daily walk and part of a larger journey that will lead us not only to a victorious life in the Spirit here in this world but to final victory in the world to come. We will witness the redemption of our bodies and the redemption of all things, which is the ultimate deliverance.

UNITED WITH CHRIST IN DEATH, BURIAL, AND RESURRECTION

Our union with the death, burial, and resurrection of Christ is the means by which we appropriate our salvation. The way of the cross is the normative method for dealing with evil and sin. We need to die to sin and not cast it out. John Sandford says it best, "Our sinful practices are not to be cast away, they are to be put to death, so that we can be transformed into the likeness of Christ."[2] We die to the old ways and are born again into the new. When we are Christ's we crucify the flesh with its lusts and affections (Gal. 5:24). The old is gone and the new is here. In 2 Cor. 5:17, the passing away of the old refers to the old creation. The verse speaks specifically to the believer, but the implications comprise all of creation. God's desire is a new heaven and a new earth. Christ came to transfigure the entire cosmos in his image. Christoformity, which is ultimately cruciformity, is God's plan. As a believer, this transformation involves spirit, soul and body, a whole new being. As believers, this transformation involves a new constitution in Christ, a new body, a new mind, a new people, and a whole new community. God's work of salvation is restoring all things to the image of Christ (Eph. 1:10; Col. 3:10). The Spirit restores the image of God daily by renewing our minds with the Word of God, as we learn who we are in Christ.

God's image is righteousness and true holiness unmarred by the disease of sin. Salvation becomes the healing and curative work of the Spirit that restores the original image of humanity. Eastern Christianity has long understood salvation therapeutically as God's cure for sin sickness. Salvation is comprehended as the wholistic healing of all things in the righteousness and holy image of God. Thus, the heart and goal of salvation is sanctification (holiness, *theosis*). Furthermore, sanctification is wrought

---

2. Sandford and Sandford, *Deliverance and Inner Healing*, 43.

through the healing work of Christ and the Spirit beginning with our deliverance from the power of sin, death and Satan. Thus, the operation of salvation involves sanctification that involves healing that involves deliverance. And as we look at the heart of salvation and its nucleus of sanctification we find the basic elements of repentance and forgiveness that lead to inner healing, deliverance, and renewal. These intertwining divine works, needless to say, are marvelous gifts given by the abundant grace of God.

REPENTANCE, FORGIVENESS, INNER HEALING

God acting sacrificially and victoriously in Christ came to atone for our sins and vanquish evil. Through the riches of his grace demonstrated on Calvary, we are forgiven of sin and set free. Mercy triumphs over judgment (James 2:13). Christ takes our judgment, as those who are both self-appointed judges and the sinful standing under judgment. He, as just judge, takes our judgment and is judged for the fulfillment of judgment that judgment may not be the final word, but by this act of mercy, the world may be forgiven.[3] The merciful offer of forgiveness lovingly calls us to repent and believe the good news. Deliverance from the judgment of evil and reconciliation with God are ours in Christ. Discussing repentance, forgiveness, healing, and deliverance, once again, we return to our fixed center, the cross. The cross is the principal instrument for deliverance legally, positionally, and experientially in our lives. At the cross, the power of sin and death is legally broken. All claims against Adam's helpless race are settled. At the cross, Jesus declared, "It is finished." In one eschatological act, sin is finished; Satan is finished; and death is finished. Through faith in the finished work of the cross, believers are positioned in Christ and have been crucified, buried, and resurrected with Christ through the work of the Holy Spirit. As believers reckon or acknowledge this completed fact (Rom. 6:11), they begin to appropriate the reality of the cross (death, burial, and resurrection) in their own experience

3. Jones, *Embodying Forgiveness*, 123–4.

through the ongoing work of the Holy Spirit. Deliverance from evil becomes a reality in their daily life. The practical implications of the finished work on the cross that results in deliverance are often realized after initial salvation when one experiences repentance, forgiveness (given or received), healing, and renewal in areas of past brokenness. It is vital to realize that past brokenness can open the door to future demonization unless there is present healing and deliverance.

At times, the practical outworking of the cross via the Spirit that results in deliverance occurs through repentance, forgiveness, identity formation in Christ, and healing of the heart. We are a new creation, complete in Christ, and yet our salvation must be worked out day to day in our lives. We are still in one sense an unfinished product, experientially speaking. Our sanctification must be worked out that involves daily surrender to the work of the Spirit, and it also means healing past brokenness and breaking old strongholds. Inner healing and deliverance specialist, John Sandford puts it this way, "Because some areas deep in our hearts have not believed and accepted the good news of our death and re-birth in Him, the fullness of his work has not yet happened for us. We are new creatures in Christ, but some of our old self-centered selfish character continues to act in its ugly old ways, as though we had not yet received the Lord."[4]

Practically, that means we are being redeemed and renewed daily. We still have brokenness and bondage issues that need to be addressed, as we draw from the finished work of Calvary. There still remains emotional and spiritual wounds that we have inherited generationally or experienced in our past that plague and impede us. Our self-image, character, personality, and relationship with God may have areas of brokenness. There may remain cracks in our soul, doors of susceptibility to temptation, sin, and demonic attacks that need to be sealed, healed, and filled with the Spirit. Much of this healing and deliverance begins with repentance.

The practice of repentance is a key spiritual discipline that leads to liberation. One Orthodox saint asks,

4. Sandford and Sandford, *Deliverance and Inner Healing*, 23.

What is repentance? It is a decisive change for the better, a breaking of the will, a turning from sin and a turning to God, or a kindling of the fire of zeal for exclusively God-pleasing things, with renunciation of the self and everything else. It is above all characterized by an extreme breaking of the will. If a person has acquired evil habits, he must now rend himself. . . Decisive and active resistance to sin comes only from hatred of it. Hatred of sin comes only from a sense of evil from it; the sense of evil from it is experienced in all its force in this painful break within repentance.[5]

With repentance, we likewise confess our sin, call it as God sees it, and name it for what it is without excuse, whitewashing, or blaming the devil.

O Father, Lord of heaven and earth, I confess to thee all the hidden and open sins of my heart and mind, which I have committed unto this present day; wherefore I beg of thee, the righteous and compassionate Judge, remission of sins and grace to sin no more.[6]

Repentance is the first blow, initially breaking the tenacious hold of the enemy on the enslaved, defeated soul. When ties are broken with a particular sin or stronghold, the devil loses his grip and control over that area in one's life. Renouncing sin and Satan pronounces a liberating claim that one will no longer relinquish one's allegiance to the enemy and his tyrannical reign. Satan's authority begins to break, as one breaks with sin, preparing the person for forgiveness, healing, deliverance, and restoration. Sin is what binds one to the devil and permits his authority to rule. When sin is broken, Satan's stronghold is broken. Repentance is "the most powerful tool we have in spiritual warfare. It removes the ground of Satan's attack."[7] Often, but not always, repentance is sufficient to bring deliverance. However, some strongholds did not develop overnight and some do not leave overnight. Deliverance is often a

---

5. Theophan, *Path of Salvation*, 92.

6. *Pocket Prayer Book for Orthodox Christians*, 43.

7. Sandford and Sandford, *Deliverance and Inner Healing*, 44.

process, involving further repentance, yielding, forgiveness, and healing over a period of God's timing. Patience, discernment, and supportive accountability are paramount in such cases.

FOLLOWING REPENTANCE IS FORGIVENESS.

> Jesus authorizes and obligates his disciples to forgive and be forgiven in God's name; more precisely, the disciples are called and enabled to do so by the power of the Holy Spirit, the Spirit of Truth. Indeed as Christians engage in practices of forgiveness, we learn from the Spirit to name truthfully the Sin and the sins that have created habits and histories of sin and evil. Hence practices of forgiveness genuinely guided by the Holy Spirit enable us to begin the slow difficult process of unlearning those habits of sin and evil.[8]

God forgives, and God requires us to forgive because that is who God is and how we live in Christ. Forgiveness received for us, and forgiveness given by us. The power to be released and to release is given to us. We are released from our captivity of unforgiveness and its guilt and shame, and we release others from our captivity of others through unforgiveness towards them. Jesus shared a powerful story of one who was released of an insufferable burden only to not release another debtor, as was done unto him. As a result of refusing to release his debtor and choosing to walk in unforgiveness, the man was imprisoned in a chamber of torment until he was willing to release his neighbor from his debt (Matt. 18:21-35).

Unrequited forgiveness and a refusal to release when we have been released can exact years of torment on the vengeful mind. Releasing and being released are vital to healing and overcoming. These practices and processes are essential to the Christian walk and are to be embodied in our life together as we live before God.[9]

8. Jones, *Embodying Forgiveness,* 131.

9. See Augsburger, *Helping People Forgive* for a thorough treatment of forgiveness in terms of theory and practice. Also for a thorough psychological analysis on the nature, practice, and benefits of forgiveness see Worthington,

L. Gregory Jones, in his rich theology of forgiveness, entitled *Embodying Forgiveness* states, "forgiveness must be embodied in a way of life, life marked by specific practices that enable us to unlearn patterns of sin, to repent for specific sins, and to foster habits of holy living."[10]

Words, acts, and patterns of forgiveness declared and appropriated have the power and authority to deliver from the deception and bondage of Satan that strangles the life of a soul with guilt and shame. Forgiveness is a potent and effective spiritual medicine that heals the deeply rooted spiritual sickness of the inner person. Countless occasions in my ministry I have witnessed persons receive and give forgiveness and be healed both physically and mentally. I have noted this breakthrough especially involving those who have been abused or traumatized and those who abuse and traumatize. Forgiveness was able to do what nothing else seemed to be able to do—work peace with God. Being released and releasing from the prison of past sins can minister an inner healing from the wreckage inflicted by iniquity. Such release begins the process of healing the broken heart, sealing the cracks of a fractured soul, and slamming the doors of opportunity where sin and Satan have insidiously seeped through past pain. In the book of James, a clear nexus is made between prayer, anointing, confessing our sins to God and each other, receiving forgiveness, and being healed:

> 14 Is anyone among you sick? Let them call the elders of the church to pray over them and anoint them with oil in the name of the Lord. 15 And the prayer offered in faith will make the sick person well; the Lord will raise them up. If they have sinned, they will be forgiven. 16 Therefore confess your sins to each other and pray for each other so that you may be healed. (NIV)

The Spirit draws us together before the Lord in prayer to share our hearts and even confess our sins against God and each other to receive release, to release, and thus to experience healing, deliverance, and renewal. In Eastern and Roman traditions such

Jr., ed., *Dimensions of Forgiveness*.

10. Jones, *Forgiveness*, 49.

anointing for inner and bodily healing holds sacramental status and is also highly valued and practiced in Pentecostal-Charismatic traditions as well. Sanctifying practices, such as repentance, forgiveness, and inner healing are instrumental to persons experiencing deliverance from sin and evil and restoration in righteousness and holiness.

DELIVERANCE: A SUBSET OF HEALING

Theologically, I have attempted to situate deliverance in the larger context of healing that is part of a larger context of salvation and sanctification. In turn, deliverance as an aspect of healing falls under the healing ministry. In Acts 10:38, Jesus "healed all of those who were oppressed of the devil." Jesus *healed* persons of demonic oppression. Deliverance involves healing of the damage inflicted by the devil to the human soul. People who have been oppressed by Satan have been deeply wounded and need to be healed, set free, and restored. Often inner healing and deliverance work go hand in hand, mending brokenness and liberating from captivity. Deliverance is a vital component of the healing ministry. The healing ministry, in restoring the human person to wholeness and to God's original image of righteousness and true holiness, is a part of the larger sanctifying ministry of the Holy Spirit, which is the heart of salvation. Sanctification cleanses and renews us completely, spirit, soul, and body. The vital work of sanctification is not optional because "without holiness no one will see the Lord (Heb. 12:14)." Yet, all sanctification, like justification, is by faith not by our own efforts.

The breadth and depth of salvation and all that it comprises in terms of sanctification, healing and deliverance, are fully realized in the work of the cross, which is once again shorthand for the death, burial, and resurrection of Christ. We are baptized into this cross and participate daily in its fellowship of suffering, death, and resurrection (Phil. 3:10). Much has been said to this point about the death side of the cross, but resurrection is the life side of the cross. The cross brings death to the old but also life to the new. The cross through resurrection completes our deliverance and healing. The power of the Spirit of holiness breaks the hold of death that is upon us and lifts us from the grave as a new creation restored in God's image. Resurrection is the source and goal, as well as the measure and capacity, of our deliverance and healing. Our healing comes from the resurrection that is it draws from the resurrection as its source. Further, our healing also begins with the resurrection (Christ's) and eschatologically leads to and ends with the resurrection (of our body and a new heaven and earth) that is our ultimate healing. So, in resurrection we are delivered from sin and death and born to eternal life, and in resurrection we are also healed completely, regardless of what realized or unrealized degree of healing or cure we experienced in this life. In the end, the resurrection is our healing. Now, we can perceive more distinctly how crucial the cross in death and resurrection is to our theology and practice of healing and deliverance.

The work of Christ on the cross co-working with the power of the Holy Spirit is God's ministry of deliverance. The church is now invited to participate in the ministry of deliverance in the name of Jesus on behalf of others. Those called to deliverance ministry serve as ministers and intercessors of this finished work of Christ on the cross on behalf of those who are held captive and desire freedom but cannot free themselves. Deliverance ministry is a priestly intercessory ministry that involves prayer, fasting, anointing, healing, and implementing the authority that Christ has given the church over sin, death, evil and Satan and all the hosts of hell.

THE LAW OF THE WILL AND AUTHORITY

Let us examine this intercessory work of deliverance in more detail. The work of intercessors is to execute and enforce the finished work of Christ, as summed up in the name of Jesus, on behalf of the demonically bound person. We are firm in our conviction that Jesus destroyed the power and authority of Satan, sin, and death on the cross. In ministering deliverance, there is no fear of the devil and his minions. Jesus has soundly defeated our enemies. We

minister deliverance from the finished work of the cross a
complete defeat of the devil. We do not grope or strive t
victory. The battle is already won. The war is over. We are merely
enforcing the victory. The deliverance team operates in the authority of Christ and executes and enforces the finished work of the
cross, where Jesus has already destroyed the works of the devil
(1 Jn. 3:8) and set the captive free. The cross provides the legal,
finished, and objective grounds for the defeat of Satan. We merely
enforce and apply daily what Christ has already accomplished. We
bind the devil and loose what the devil has bound with the keys
(authority) of the kingdom (Matt. 16:19; 18:18).

Those ministering enforce deliverance in the name of Jesus,
the name that is given as a power of attorney to believers to act on
Christ's behalf in his power and authority. Intercessors co-work
with the leading and power of the Spirit to break the powers of
darkness that are controlling the bound person. The individual is
then led to yield to the delivering work of the cross. In ministering
deliverance, it is paramount to understand the power of the name
of Jesus. The saving work of God is embodied fully in the Son
of Man and represented by the name of Jesus. When we in faith
address Jesus by name, we are calling on the full person, work,
and authority of Christ to minister deliverance and salvation. The
name of Jesus is the only name given to the world for salvation
(Acts 4:12). All are called to bow at the name of Jesus (Phil. 4:10).
In Jesus' name his disciples shall overthrow, trample underfoot,
and cast out demons. There is power in the name of Jesus. Persons bound are called to repent and renounce forever their former
practices and confess the Lordship of Christ.

As in the ancient baptismal liturgy and covenant of the early
church, believers are called to renounce Satan, his power, and his
works. Individuals are reminded that they willfully gave into temptation and sin. They need to recover their will by acknowledging
that they freely chose to sin, and now they can freely choose to
surrender to Christ. There is no deliverance in blaming the devil
for their own willful surrender to the power of the enemy. Now,
they need to cooperate with God's grace and choose the truth

and right standing before God by surrendering to Christ. This act of turning is an essential part of repentance. Persons gain hope by recognizing as they once yielded their lives as instruments of sin, now they can yield their lives as instruments of righteousness Rom. 6:12-19).

By the grace and power of God, the captive need to recapture their will. Recapturing the will begins by persons acknowledging that they willfully chose to rebel, but now by grace they can willfully choose to resist sin and Satan and obey God. Deliverance is appropriated based on reversing the law of the will and authority. This law determines and governs the nature and degree of bondage. What I am calling the "law of the will and authority" is that whatever sin one submits one's will to, then that sin or practice has authority over one's will. Also to the degree that one submits one's will to a particular sin, then to that degree that sin has control over one's life. Jesus, said in John 8:34, "Very truly I tell you, everyone who sins is a slave to sin." 2 Peter 2:19 (NLT) indicates, "For you are a slave to whatever controls you."

Conversely, to the degree one submits to the Lordship of Christ to that degree Christ has authority over the person and manifests his authority. Again, to the degree one submits to sin, to that degree sin has authority and control over one's life. The degree of control in one's everyday life can in part be "measured" by the nature of the sinful practice or stronghold and the duration, frequency, and intensity of the practice. By way of illustration, we note the increased degree of influence in the life of the addict as a function of generations, frequency, duration, and intensity of use of a particular substance. The degree of bondage of one who beer binges for a weekend for the first time is in a different place then the alcoholic who has been drunk daily with hard liquor for over thirty years, though both conditions are not welcomed. The degree of demonic influence over the one who looks at another person with lust on two or three occasions is quite different than the degree of demonic influence over the one who has lusted over a person time and again, regularly fantasized about it, and eventually committed adultery daily with that person over a ten-year period.

The demonic influence is greater in the case of the latter than of the former. The degree of demonic influence becomes a function of generational sin, frequency (daily), duration (ten years), and intensity (from thought to act). The law of habit strengthens the chains of sin. Deliverance involves the breaking of chains, the liberating of the will, and the reversal of authority.

In deliverance, God is reversing the control and authority over the will from Satan and sin to Christ and obedience. This process begins by God empowering individuals to recover their will in repentance and to own their compliance to sin and then to yield to Christ in that area. The intercessors begin to drive out the devil in the name of Jesus, following repentance. Persons bound need to demonstrate a willingness to be set free, although it is God who supplies the grace and power for the heavy lifting of repentance and deliverance.

In the character, fruit, and Spirit of Christ, the intercessors are encouraged to minister deliverance with both humility and boldness. Special attention should be paid to the pastoral ministry and the pastoral moment (timing) of deliverance. The deliverance team needs to be sensitive to all pastoral issues that arise specifically around protecting the integrity, dignity, confidentiality, and will of the person who will be receiving prayer. Also proper prayer preparation prior to deliverance sessions and intentional discipleship sessions following deliverance sessions are imperative to full restoration of those receiving deliverance (See chapter 9).

Practices of inner healing and belief and identity formation are essential before and after deliverance.[11] In fact, many demonic strongholds break easily following such careful and prayerful preparation. Remember, all cracks in the soul where the devil can gain a foothold need to be sealed and the low areas built up with the Word, so that the house is repaired and can keep out sin and be filled with the Spirit less the devil return back sevenfold. Rigorous

11. See Bellini, *Truth Therapy* for other strategies of inner healing, belief and identity formation, and discipleship for pre and post deliverance. Repentance, forgiveness (giving and receiving), and accepting the truth concerning one's identity in Christ are indispensible practices for receiving deliverance.

catechesis and belief formation that shape Christian identity are essential to preventing relapse and more importantly fostering growth and maturity in Christ.[12] Belief formation begins in the Word of God and identity formation begins with the personal application of truth from God's Word that declares that we are a new creation in Christ and promises us that we can do all things through Christ who gives us strength. Vessels that have been delivered and emptied and have had cracks sealed need to be filled with the Spirit and the Word of God. Romans 12:1-2 claims transformation in our lives occurs when our minds are renewed with the Word of God. Discipleship, becoming disciplined learners and followers of Jesus Christ, begins when we learn our new identity in Christ.

12. A sampling of works in Christian belief and identity formation related to deliverance, include Anderson's *Bondage Breakers, Who I am in Christ, Victory Over the Darkness* and Bellini's *Truth Therapy,* Richard Foster's *Devotional Classics: Selected Readings for Individuals and Groups,* and Dallas Willard's *Renovation of the Heart, Hearing God, and the Divine Conspiracy,* Sondra Matthaei's *Making Disciples Faith Formation in the Wesleyan Tradition,* Derek Krueger's *Liturgical Subjects: Christian Ritual, Biblical Narrative, and the Formation of the Self in Byzantium,* Anne Streaty Wimberly's, *Faith Formation in the black Tradition,* among others.

5

An Integrative Approach to Healing and Deliverance

"Therefore every teacher of the law who has become a disciple in the kingdom of heaven is like the owner of a house who brings out of his storeroom new treasures as well as old."—Matthew 13:52.

A TALE OF TWO CASES

SOME OF MY DESIRE to propose an integrated model for healing and deliverance comes from my experience as a pastor in the local church. Let me share a tale of two cases from my days as an inner-city pastor that sums up my experience with congregants struggling with mental health and deliverance in the local church. The first is the story of Lisa (not her real name). Lisa had weathered an abusive relationship with her father for years, and the pattern was repeating itself in her five-year marriage. From her late teens, into her late twenties, and throughout her marriage, she received regular counseling and was prescribed various regimens of meds for depression and anxiety. Lisa was occasionally suicidal and often had panic attacks and debilitating episodes of spiraling despair and depression. Counseling and meds seemed to help only minimally over those ten plus years. She complained of minimal relief from symptoms.

Following a major episode of depression and anxiety that culminated in an attempted suicide, Lisa was introduced to our church through a common friend. My wife and I began to dedicate much time to Lisa, praying and studying the scriptures together. We also anointed her, laid hands on her, and prayed for her full inner healing and deliverance regularly. Through what we perceived to be the teaching of the scriptures, inner healing and deliverance prayer, and the work of the Spirit, Lisa began to experience God's touch and changed her perspective on her depression. Previously, she imagined that she could never escape from this suffocating tomb of despair. Now inspired by hope, she began to see the possibility of freedom and a new life and grew daily through intentional discipleship. Where counseling and meds alone reached an impasse, Lisa seemed to find relief by finding peace with God, while continuing regular treatment and counseling.

Eighteen years later, Lisa has grown and matured in Christ. She is committed to participating in the life of the local church, attends small group discipleship, and is occasionally involved in outreach ministry. Lisa also has regular devotional time that involves prayer and studying the scriptures. She has found victory over her depression by depending on Christ as her sufficiency. Lisa is no longer suicidal and does not experience the panic attacks or the overwhelming bouts of depression. She takes a minimal dose of Prozac for maintenance but no longer feels the need for counseling. God not only began to heal her of the debilitating impact from anxiety-depressive disorder but also gave her the power to address her dysfunctional marriage. The couple attended counseling for a season and found the grace and strength to make some life changing decisions in their marriage. Today, though certainly not perfect or without trials, Lisa lives as a new creation in Christ, walking day to day on the path of wholeness.

Jeff (not his real name) was a leader in the young adult group of the church. While in leadership, he was also attending the local university where he was majoring in Physics. Jeff was known by family, church leaders, and peers as an intelligent, highly functioning, and a deeply spiritual young man of God. One semester was memorably more challenging than the others. He was carrying a much heavier course load than usual and entered into upper level courses from his major. Jeff continued in leadership in the church's young adult group that semester. On top of these responsibilities, Jeff faced additional extenuating circumstances. His parents were going through some financial difficulty and began to argue constantly and even discuss divorce.

Jeff noticed that his performance in school was slipping. His test scores were lower than normal. Focusing in class and doing homework became a tiring chore. He found his mind racing when he attempted to concentrate on his work. Jeff found himself underperforming and became impatient with himself and others and was easily irritated by the smallest challenges. After a few weeks of the same pattern of behavior, Jeff found himself struggling to eat and to sleep at night. He began to spiral into ruminations of hopelessness and despair. These drastic changes were overwhelming. He wondered if he would ever be himself again. Jeff kept telling himself to "just snap out of it", but it was not that simple. Devotional time and prayer seemed to help for short periods until the pressures of the day would descend once again swallowing his stability and peace of mind. Simple day-to-day functioning became an insurmountable task. Jeff asked for prayer from church leadership and "deliverance" teams, but there was no significant breakthrough after much prayer. Nothing seemed to work.

Feeling helpless, Jeff confided in his mother who made an appointment with the family physician, who in turn made a referral to a Christian therapist. Jeff was diagnosed with clinical depression. He was also put on an average dose of Zoloft. He spent the next few months in counseling talking through the many circumstances that seemed to be caving in on him. Jeff discovered that opening up and verbalizing his internal battles made his struggles manageable, while at the same time enabling him to expel bottled up anger and to unload much of the burden of worry and fear that was weighing him down. Through counseling and talking out his concerns, it was not long after that Jeff began to feel himself again. The medication alleviated symptoms, while the talk therapy equipped him with skills to restructure some of the fearful thinking that gripped him. Medication and counseling together with regular spiritual disciplines enabled him to better cope with the many struggles he had been facing at this tumultuous time in his life. After almost a year, Jeff was back on track at school, at home and with his walk with Christ. His depression was not cured but managed, and Jeff felt he could be himself again.

To summarize, Lisa was receiving counseling and meds but also needed to invest in her spiritual life. Jeff was committed spiritually. He prayed regularly and was walking with Christ, but he needed medication coupled with good counseling to experience relief. In both cases, an unnecessary form of dualism got the best of them. Clearly, every case cannot be so simple, and even these cases surely had other factors that contributed to both the depression and the relief of symptoms. However, I could share many other similar stories how parishioners benefited from different integrative approaches to divine healing and mental health, especially cases of schizophrenia in which deliverance sessions failed. I do not believe that Lisa and Jeff's stories of depression and anxiety are unique in the local church.

Neuropsychiatric disorders, which include depression and anxiety, are the leading cause of disability in the U.S., followed by cardiovascular and circulatory diseases.[1] Neuropsychiatric disorders, such as depression and anxiety, are also the leading risk factors in suicide.[2] In 2009, suicide was the third leading cause of death for young people ages fifteen to twenty-four. In this age group, suicide accounted for 14.4 percent of all deaths in 2009.[3] The National Institute of Mental Health reports that an "estimated

1. "U.S. Leading Categories of Diseases/Disorders," National Institute of Mental Health, 2010.

2. "Suicide in America: Frequently Asked Questions," National Institute of Mental Health.

3. "Leading Cause of Death Ages 18-65 in the U.S.," National Institute of Health, 2007.

43.7 million adults aged 18 or older in the U.S. suffer with Any Mental Illness (AMI) in the past year," representing 18.6 percent of all U.S. adults.[4] Mental disorders are prevalent and on the rise, but possibly an equally disturbing reality is that many disorders are not being treated. For example, the twelve-month prevalence of any anxiety disorder in the U.S. among adults is 18.1 percent. Of that 18.1 percent, only 36.9 percent are receiving any treatment, and of that 36.9 percent, only 34.3 percent, or 12.7 percent overall, are receiving minimally adequate treatment.[5]

Are members of the church being diagnosed and properly treated for mental illness, or do their Christian cultural beliefs hinder treatment and recovery? Surely, prayer and scriptural study are central disciplines to our formation in Christian faith and practice and equip us to face life's struggles. The problem is that half of a segment of the Christian population holds that medication and /or therapy are not necessary to the treatment of mental illness. Such a conclusion flies in the face of medical science, which claims that therapy and medication can be up to 90 percent effective in treating the symptoms of mental disorders. Furthermore, such dualistic thinking seems to bifurcate truth into the truths of science and the truths of theology, implying that medicine is not a gift from God, or that God and medical science are necessarily diametrically opposed. Is it wise to not apply the entire God given resources available for healing, including resources from both faith and science? [6]

The study done by LifeWay Research indicates that mental health in general is a taboo subject in the church. The study polled 1000 Protestant pastors, 355 Protestant Americans diagnosed with an acute mental illness, among them were 200 churchgoers, 207 Protestant family members of people with acute mental illness, and fifteen experts on spirituality and mental illness. Again,

4. "Any Mental Illness Among U.S. Adults," National Institute of Mental Health.

5. "Any Anxiety Order Among Adults," National Institute of Health.

6. For example, Matthew Stanford, professor of Psychology and Neuroscience at Baylor University, argues for the balance of theology and science and the right use of psychiatric medicine, counseling, and faith in much of his work, including *Grace for the Afflicted*.

does the church have the resources to inform, direct, support, and minister healing to those with mental illnesses in their fold? The research claims that:

> Most Protestant senior pastors (66 percent) seldom speak to their congregation about mental illness. About one in six pastors (16 percent) speak about mental illness once a year. And about a quarter of pastors (22 percent) are reluctant to help those who suffer from acute mental illness because it takes too much time. [7] Pastors want to help but do not feel trained and prepared to do so. They often lack human resources and an informed and practical plan of ministry that addresses the complexity of mental health in their congregations. For example, "only a quarter of churches (27 percent) have a plan to assist families affected by mental illness according to pastors. And only 21 percent of family members are aware of a plan in their church."[8] Only 14 percent of the churches surveyed have a counselor, staff person or leader trained to recognize mental illness.[9] Although the church is ill equipped to minister with persons suffering from mental disorders, "family members (65 percent) and those with mental illness (59 percent) want their church to talk openly about mental illness, so the topic will not be a taboo."[10]

The research is clear that pastors are not tackling this tough subject, and one of the reasons besides being ill-equipped may be that "about a quarter of pastors (23 percent), say they have also experienced some kind of mental illness, while 12 percent say they received a diagnosis for a mental health condition."[11] The study indicates that pastors are both reluctant to get an official diagnosis and reluctant to talk about their own struggle. Such inhibition may contribute to a pastor's reticence to address issues around mental

7. Smietana, "Mental Illness Remains Taboo Topic for Many Pastors."
8. Smietana, "Mental Illness Remains Taboo Topic for Many Pastors."
9. Smietana, "Mental Illness Remains Taboo Topic for Many Pastors."
10. Smietana, "Mental Illness Remains Taboo Topic for Many Pastors."
11. Smietana, "Mental Illness Remains Taboo Topic for Many Pastors."

health. In any case, mental illness remains a silent killer in the church.

MY EXPERIENCE

Since 1988 I have ministered in a variety of capacities in the life of the church, including deliverance and healing ministry, prison ministry, campus ministry, evangelistic and revivalistic work and campaigns, conference and seminar speaking, church planting, CEO of a 501c3, and a senior pastor of several local churches. As an ordained Elder in the United Methodist Church, I am currently serving in an extension appointment beyond the local church as professor of Evangelization and Church Renewal at United Theological Seminary in Dayton, Ohio. Out of my thirty plus years in ministry, one of the most consistent problems I have encountered is the staggering number of persons in the church that struggle with mental health issues, particularly depression and anxiety, especially cases undiagnosed and untreated.

I have observed many suffering with depression and anxiety even though they pray, seek deliverance, believe the scriptures for healing, and participate in the full life of the church. Being an active, committed Christian does not exempt one from suffering from mental disorders. Confirming the Lifeway study, I found that many expected a change apart from receiving medical treatment. In my ministry, some were healed of mental disorders directly and solely by "the hand of God", in terms of healing without treatment. At least, in the short term, I detected a subsiding of symptoms. I am not sure of the long term for some persons did not remain in our local church long enough to track. Yet, I encountered many more who suffered needlessly without remission when going undiagnosed and untreated. In the church, mental disorder seems to be everywhere but rarely addressed. Many suffer needlessly because they lack knowledge. Admittedly, in other cases, I have encountered persons who were receiving medical treatment and counseling but did not believe that God could heal them through prayer, as in the case of Lisa. In some of the other cases, persons were simply treatment resistant.

These disorders are rarely "curable" by any known treatment, although healing surely occurs. Clearly, I am making a distinction between curing and healing. Curing would involve instant or eventual, total, and lifelong eradication of any and every[12] mental disorder or disability and all related symptoms without any relapse or further treatment of any type that a person would experience. Many of the churches that I have pastored are "charismatic," as am I, meaning they aggressively believe in the gifts of the Spirit, including divine healing and deliverance. Faith, anointing with oil, laying on of hands, and prayer for healing are regular liturgical practices in such churches. Healings frequently occur. More so, integrated approaches that involve intentional discipleship, inner healing and deliverance administered along side the work of the other health care professions are most effective and have yielded stunning results. I, along with the congregations I pastored, witnessed all types of healing, corroborated by medical professionals. Surely, God can do all things, but rarely have I witnessed lifelong mental disorders or intellectual disabilities be fully reversed and cured without the need for medication and remain cured over a long period of time as documented and corroborated by the medical community. I have witnessed healing ministries make claims of curing while either in denial or without corroboration from the medical community or not following-up long-term on the individual. Healing and deliverance ministries need to be realistic about the persistent challenge of mental disorders. A comprehensive approach found in God's prevenient grace that utilizes the best resources of science and the Spirit is the most effective means towards wholeness. However, the church often shuns God's prevenient and common grace offered through the medical community. The church and science have a longstanding unresolved feud that carries over into the pews.

12. Comorbidity frequently occurs with mental disorders. Rarely does one mental disorder manifest alone without other symptoms and disorders present.

WHY THE CHURCH WON'T TAKE ITS MEDS

Mental health issues are complex in terms of etiology, diagnosis, pathogenesis, treatment and prognosis. Various fields in research and care need to collaborate to treat the multi-dimensional nature of mental disorders. Often Christian dualism, "folk worldviews" and "folk theologies" that polarize "Christian" truth and the discoveries and truths of the sciences are suspicious of any cooperation between the two. Scrutiny and wariness have characterized their dialogue for centuries.[13] We note this beginning more acutely with the groundbreaking discoveries made during the scientific revolution. Breakthroughs in astronomy made by Copernicus, Kepler, and Galileo undermined the prevailing account of the universe held by the church. The church has since had a bitter rivalry with the sciences, which is ironic since many of the key ideas of the scientific revolution were generated out of a Christian worldview.

Nevertheless, key scientific innovations made during the centuries following the scientific revolution seemed to undercut a literalist reading of scripture, resulting in the polarization of faith and reason that played out among debating fundamentalists and modernists. Strict ratio-empiricism has doggedly competed with faith as the valid source for epistemic authority in the modern age. The battle escalated in the nineteenth and twentieth centuries as the scientific method was applied consistently to the investigation of the origin, authenticity, and veracity of scripture. With the advent and standardizing of biblical criticism over the last few centuries, science challenged the foundational role that a certain construal of scripture had played in theological epistemology and faith formation for many evangelicals and fundamentalist Christians. As a result, the church has often taken a defensive posture against science and the defeater role science has taken on in theological epistemology.[14]

13. See Brooke, *Science and Religion*.

14. Christianity has wrestled with science from the time of Copernicus and Galileo to Darwin and following namely due to the tension between a literalist reading of Scripture and the findings of science and thus a crisis in epistemic authority. For a balanced treatment of these and other issues see *Blackwell*

In the midst of this rivalry, laity in the pews feel forced to choose from the false dichotomy of faith or reason. They ask themselves, "Do we trust the dogma of the church or the findings of science," or "Do we trust the Bible or critical reason?" In terms of mental health, not only is there a general distrust of science on the part of the church, but there is also a very specific distrust of psychology and its related fields. For some, it is an either/or end game. Depending on psychology and psychiatry in certain folk worldviews and theologies signifies 'not trusting in God for healing.'[15] For radical "faith healing" type of Christians, the two mutually exclude each other. The mindset is if one is ultimately trusting God for healing, then one cannot expect healing to come from a doctor or medicine. The latter is an act of unbelief.

For others, psychology, and specifically psychiatry, is considered more of an art than a science, especially when diagnosing and treating mental disorders. For example, there is not an objective, biological test that can be taken that detects and diagnoses depression or anxiety, as there is for diabetes or cancer. A concrete, visible diagnosis is not available, often lending to distrust. Once a diagnosis is made from the DSM-5 based on symptomatology, effective medical treatment is often hit or miss based on the right medication and the patient's makeup, which is the case with all diseases and treatments at some level but not as great as with "subjective" disorders. Other psychological factors such as relying on medication, fear of chemical dependence, over-medication, and the notion that pharmaceuticals and the medical field have become a self-justifying big business that is all about money have contributed to society's and the church's general skepticism towards the field. All of these hesitations are legitimate concerns that need our continual attention.

However, regarding psychology and mental illness, the church is most challenged by the prevailing folk preconception

---

Companion to Science and Christianity, (Wiley-Blackwell, 2012).

15. The view that visiting a doctor and taking medication is contrary to faith and is a form of unbelief is still common among Pentecostal and Charismatics in the world today.

that Christians do not have to face or deal with mental disorders *eo ipso* they are Christians. My pastoral experience has been that believers erroneously think that because they are "Christians", or "saved", or "Spirit-filled," that they cannot, should not, do not, or will not have mental health issues. Somehow, they feel divinely entitled and that having Christ in their life exempts them from facing this challenge. Thus, in many cases, mental illness goes undiagnosed, underdiagnosed, untreated, or undertreated. This erroneous preconception generates both misunderstanding and stigma in regards to mental disorders. Having a mental disorder means you have sinned or are not a believer, or in order to keep a Christian testimony, you have to remain in denial about the problem. Such misapprehension also enables these disabilities to remain hidden, undetected and hence potent and menacing. Fortunately, some Christian leaders have been courageous to shine the light in their churches and on the pressing issue of mental health. LifeWay research recently under Ed Stetzer and other popular leaders like Rick Warren Pastor of Saddleback Church have been instrumental in leading and educating pastors and the laity of the church about mental health issues.[16]

In citing the research from the LifeWay study, I am not only pointing out the church's neglect to address effectively the matters, but I am also highlighting the imperative for a wholistic or integrative approach that brings the best of the sciences and faith together to dialogue. A reductive, materialist approach or a purely ratio-empirical approach to reality can limit one's discovery of truth as much as a precritical fundamentalist worldview. Rather than utilizing approaches that limit methodology, a "truth-quest" method, or a method that seeks truth through a variety of disciplines and a variety of methodologies can be effective at bringing science and religion together for a further conversation, as scientists such as

---

16. The suicide of Rick Warren's 27-year-old son in 2013 ignited church and public awareness of the shadow of mental illness and its connection with suicide.

Ian Barbour, Arthur Peacocke and John Polkinghorne among others have pointed out.[17]

RELIGION AND SCIENCE: WILL THE TWAIN EVER MEET?

What resources can both theology and science afford in order to assist in health and healing? How can "scientific" truth collaborate with "theological" truth? Ultimately, "all truth is God's truth," paraphrasing St. Augustine from *On Christian Doctrine*. So, I assume the possibility, not always probable though, that theology and science can find a point of contact and be in dialogue, and even, at times, be compatible and complement each other in their work. Theology and science do not have to be mutually exclusive. The truths of theology may be compatible with the truths of science, and at times they can collaborate in their efforts.

However, in claiming, "All truth is God's truth," I am not claiming several things. I am not claiming that all truths are salvific. Knowing Newton's Universal Law of Gravitation, $F = G\,(m1m2)/r2$, will not bring you the salvation that is only found in Jesus Christ. Although there may be truths in science that are not mentioned in scripture, such truths do not trump scripture in terms of informing our salvation, faith and practice. The scriptures, interpreted by the great tradition of the church, are theological in nature and are our sufficient guide for salvation. Further, not all truths address the same subject, have the same effect, or are equal in significance. The primary subject matter of theology is God, while the primary subject matter of science is the universe. Knowledge of the former comes by faith and brings eternal peace. Knowledge of the latter comes by reason and brings temporal certainty.

In addition, in claiming, "All truth is God's truth," I am not claiming that truths are in ultimate conflict. The truths of science, as in the laws of nature, are not in conflict with the truths of faith, as in the will and commandments of God. In the mind of God all

17. Polkinghorne, *Science and Religion in Quest of Truth*.

truths are networked somehow, including the truths of quantum mechanics and the truths of Christology, even though I may not understand how they relate. A posture that assumes these two fields are inherently in opposition is not necessary, although their methodologies and objects of inquiry may differ.

In the academy of Thomas Aquinas' day, theology was called the "queen of sciences". Sacred or dogmatic theology was queen over the *trivium* of grammar, logic and rhetoric as well as over the *quadrivium* of arithmetic, geometry, music and astronomy. With the advent of the scientific revolution, the dogmatic use of the scientific method, and the development of the modern hard and soft sciences, theology would no longer be considered a science due to its object and method of inquiry. Prussian philosopher Immanuel Kant demonstrated for the Enlightenment that God was not a proper object of scientific or rational inquiry, beyond the moral demand of duty.[18]

Although I do not concur with Kant's unqualified dismissal of metaphysics, I believe that theology and science rightfully developed into separate fields with distinct methodologies and objects of inquiry. Even if theology could be claimed in some unique way to be a science, it would be a science of a different nature than the hard sciences. Theology studies the creator and the creator's relation to creation. Science studies creation or the universe and its contents and laws of operation. In terms of method, theology employs faith and subordinate reason, and science employs reason and a subordinate faith. Theology does not always make good science, nor does science always make good theology. It is evident that the two disciplines can function independently. Although theology is not science, and science is not theology, and the two are not to be confused, they are not necessarily mutually exclusive in all of their claims. They both seek the truth and ultimate reality, and they both seek truth about our world and our lives. There seems to be conjunctive inquiry around the ultimate nature of things. Scientists, like Arthur Peacocke, stress the need for both theology and science to operate out of a common metaphysics of

18. See Kant's *Critique of Pure Reason*.

creation to discover convergence and points of contact and conversation. Let us briefly continue in this vein and survey some models of science and religion.

SCIENCE AND RELIGION: FRIENDS OR FOES?

Examining the relationship between science and religion has become its own field of inquiry. The physicist and philosophy of religion professor Ian Barbour was one of the pioneers that sought to integrate science and religion. In his classic work *Religion and Science,* he poses four models for understanding the possible relationship between the two fields: conflict, independence, dialogue and integration.[19] Finding conflict in religion and science is not too difficult. Surely, there are numerous points where the two are in conflict, such as in a literalist reading of the creation account in Genesis versus the latest string theory of cosmology.[20] In terms of independence, it remains fairly unproblematic to identify different domains, languages, methods, and objects of inquiry that religion and science hold, allowing each to operate rather freely of the other. One can observe and understand the operations of gravity without faith in God, as well as one can understand one's sins are forgiven without the proof of science.

Barbour cites an example of science-religion independence found in George Lindbeck's classical work *The Nature of Doctrine.* The cultural-linguistic model of doctrine illustrates how religions can work independently of each other and independently of other fields like science.[21] Each religion and even each field of study like science, functions as a culture with its own language and is intelligible only to those who participate in the narrative of that particular language-game. Doctrine functions as "rules of

19. Barbour, *Religion and Science,* 77–103.

20. There are obviously various readings of the first few chapters of Genesis. For example see *Genesis: History, Fiction, or Neither?: Three Views on the Bible's Earliest Chapters,* Halton et al., 2015

21. Lindbeck, *Nature of Doctrine: Religion and Theology in a Postliberal Age.*

discourse" within a religious tradition, like Ludwig Wittgenstein's language games where each game is held together and functions internally with its own set of rules. In this sense, one can speak of doctrine as a cultural-linguistic project within a religious tradition particularly and independently of truth claims from another religious tradition or field of study. Each cultural-linguistic system is independent and incommensurate with the next.

Although Barbour believes that independence is a good place to start, it is not where we want to finish. Independence affirms and preserves the integrity of each field and the "distinct character of each enterprise," but it leaves our inquiry incomplete.[22] Science asks questions about cosmological origins that theology addresses in its account of creation, and theology probes the nature of God's handiwork that science investigates physically in macro and micro detail. At the boundaries and limits that define the distinctions of each field, there are ontological questions that one field proposes but cannot answer and may be addressed in the scope of the other field. Barbour identifies both methodological parallels and nature-inspired spirituality that are shared by both theology and science and reveal some commonality lending for further fruitful dialogue and even integration.

We have grounds for dialogue. Following the Enlightenment and the impact of reason and science on the world and the church, it would be shortsighted of our theology at the least to not be in dialogue with science. The church's condemnation of Copernicus reminds us of the fate of a theology that refuses dialogue with science. Such religion blindly ignores the truth and is left in ignorance. Similarly, science cannot simply dismiss the claims of theology because the object of its inquiry and methodology are different. Basic belief in God can be considered justified and as rational as any other basic belief.[23] Dialogue acknowledges that each field of study has a unique perspective and contribution to understanding the overall big picture.

22. Barbour, *Religion*, 88.
23. See Alvin Plantinga's trilogy on *Warrant*.

Concerning dialogue, there are levels of explanation to any given phenomena, and each field can provide an informed perspective based on its unique theories, frameworks, and methodologies. Dialogue between fields opens up the door to exploration, exchange, and a more comprehensive understanding of the problem and hopefully the solution. For example, in the case of mental health, etiology and symptoms are not always singular and clear cut. A faith perspective offers insight into spiritual causality and spiritual solutions. While pharmacology, if needed, may speak to the chemical aspects of the problem, therapy, depending on the type, may address cognitive-behavioral issues. Of course, there are a variety of perspectives on the compatibility of Christianity and psychology to consider, which is a different subject entirely.[24]

The dialogue model of religion and science allows for mutual conversation, learning, and understanding between the disciplines, discovering and interpreting similarities and dissimilarities, continuity and discontinuity, congruence and incongruence and the consequences that follow. In dialogue, both communities may seek points of contact and correlation for further engagement and cooperation in search of a greater truth and a larger vision of reality. Such contact and correlation can occur at the limits of both domains where boundaries are formed and boundary questions arise, and at times these boundaries may join together and even form a hinge for both fields to be joined.

For science, the boundaries are often metaphysical and involve ultimate questions of origin, causality, meaning, purpose, and finality. For theology, the boundaries are often natural and experimental or empirical and involve questions of experience, operation, function, and practice. At times, philosophy can serve as a mediator between theology (philosophical theology or philosophy of religion) and science (philosophy of science), providing a theoretical and conceptual bridge between the two, i.e. metaphysics. Barbour cites natural theology, a theology of nature, and

---

24. For an introduction to various perspectives on psychology and Christianity, especially "a levels of explanation view" and "an integration view" see Eric L. Johnson, ed., *Psychology and Christianity: Five Views.*

especially metaphysics as a site for dialogue and further integration. He claims, "A more systematic integration can occur if both science and religion contribute to a coherent world view elaborated in a comprehensive metaphysics."[25]In seeking a compatible metaphysical system, Barbour endorses a type of critical realism that functions as a bridge between science and religion.[26] In his estimation, critical realism avoids the problems of naïve realism but refuses to fall into the postmodern traps of instrumentalism and idealism that deny an external world and claim our theories of the universe are merely "human constructs," "calculating devices" (instrumentalism) or solely conceptual products (idealism). [27] Critical realism holds to a "real," external world but notes that our comprehension of the universe is partial and relies referentially on metaphors, models, and analogical language, all three being conducive vehicles for both science and religion.

John Polkinghorne has also developed an integrative model of theology and science that utilizes the bridge of critical realism. The model recognizes three stages of complexity in the universe: first, the laws of nature that support the causal structure of the universe; second, human agency and freewill; third, divine providence and interaction.[28] The interface between stages is bridged by causal joints that we hypothesize are covered by frameworks such as, quantum mechanics, chaos dynamics, the analogy of being, kenosis, apophasis, or some other theory. The truth is that each of these areas is being explored, and we do not have incorrigible epistemic certainty in regards to them. Polkinghorne, and I concur,

25. Barbour, *Religion*, 103. Barbour preliminarily considers Thomism and finally Whiteheadian process philosophy as viable systems of metaphysics through which science and religion can converse and even integrate.

26. Other theologian-scientists who turn to critical realism as a bridge between religion and science are Arthur Peacocke, John Polkinghorne, and Robert Russell, and philosopher-scientist Michael Polanyi, among others. See, Paul Allen's *Ernan McMullin and Critical Realism in the Science-Theology Dialogue* for a comparative analysis of the critical realism of Barbour, Peacocke, and Polkinghorne.

27. Barbour, *When Science Meets Religion*, 74.

28. Polkinghorne, *Science and Religion in Quest of Truth*, 85–90.

maintains that an integrative model that makes room for all three domains best explains our full understanding and experience of reality without removing, reducing, or explaining away any of the three. Furthermore, neither is it possible to parse causality into three simple compartments since the casual structure is too complex and entangled for such an oversimplifying task.[29]

However, because we cannot totally explain how things occur does not mean that they do not occur. The epistemological fallacy and modern notion that unless we know everything (about a matter), then we cannot know anything (about a matter) is surely a fallacy that begs for epistemic humility. Physicist and philosopher Michael Polanyi has contributed richly to this conversation with his proposal that all knowledge to some degree is personal knowledge.[30] The thesis of his work is that all knowledge involves the personal participation of the knower. All data, observation, inquiry, and experience are theory, interpretation, and value laden not only in religion but also in science. Personal and community commitment and participation are integral to the construction of knowledge. Thus, there is no clear-cut separation of reason from faith and faith from reason. We make a fiduciary commitment to our inquiry and to our construction of knowledge. Belief is developmental to knowledge and practice. There is no pure and total science as touted by the dogma of scientism.

With epistemic humility undergirding the work of dialogue, the possibility of integration can emerge. Theology and science can work together in some form and find some degree of compatibility and even integration. In dialogue, it is vital not to bifurcate the two domains of theology and science so radically as to cut off all conversation, as if the two necessarily mutually exclude each other. Although they explore different worlds with some overlap between the fields, theology and science also have a degree of methodological overlap that invites hospitable discourse.

In examining the possibility of dialogue and integration, many theologian-scientists posit the bridge of critical realism as

29. Polkinghorne, *Science and Religion*, 89.

30. Polanyi, *Personal Knowledge*.

a way forward, though it is not without its critics and problems. Overall, Barbour's work in critical realism and typology is one of the most enduring and frequently used for its simplicity and scope. Others have either built upon or responded to Barbour with differing typologies. Following Barbour in 1981, Arthur Peacocke offered an eightfold typology comparing and contrasting the two fields in four areas, *approaches, languages, attitudes,* and *objects.* In these areas, the "relation between science and theology can be construed as either positive and reconciling and so as mutually interacting, or as negative and non-interacting."[31]

In 1985, Nancey Murphy borrowed Niebuhr's classic fivefold typology of Christ and culture and revised it into a science and religion typology. More recently, John Haught in *Science and Religion,* modifying Barbour, constructs a fourfold typology of conflict, contrast, contact, and confirmation. Further Robert Russell cites more recently the developments of Willem Drees' nine-fold typology, Philip Hefner's six-fold typology, and Ted Peter's eightfold typology, among others, as attempts to build on or refine Barbour's work.[32] The space and aim of this study is not to examine and critique each typology but to acknowledge the critical work being done in this area, recognizing the possibility of dialogue between theology and science and even the possibility of a soft integration where there are points of contact (Haught). Integration is a "hard" notion and seems to involve a combining of two fields into one field. Many questions arise? What is the nature of combining? What is the nature of the two combined into one? Do the two fields that are combined merge and lose distinction in their integration? If two becoming one is hard integration, then I do not deem integration possible due to the distinct nature of the disciplines. But out of dialogue, if the two fields can uniquely contribute out of their domain and participate and function together to explain and address a particular issue, drawing from each other, yet remaining distinct, then I think such a soft integration that is participatory and provisional may be possible.

31. Peacocke, *Theology for a Scientific Age,* 20.
32. See Russell, "Dialogue, Science and Theology."

Dialogue and soft integration may be possible in the fields of deliverance and mental health, i.e. a wholistic approach. Barbour claims methodological parallels (similarities and differences) for religion and science. Both make cognitive claims from a "hypothetico-deductive method and contextualist-historicist framework". Both organize observations and experiences through analogical models expressed in metaphorical language. In the case of mental health, both science and religion can serve transformative purposes, changing the thoughts and life of an individual. The obvious difference is that science proposes theory derived from empirical evidence, while theology works with revelation derived from God. However, through points of contact, the two disciplines can enter into conversation and investigate how to work together.

THE POSSIBILITY OF AN INTEGRATIVE APPROACH TO MENTAL HEALTH IN CHRISTIAN MINISTRY

Let us attempt to apply Barbour's notion of integration and methodological parallels and Haught's view of contact to the conversation between mental health and Christian theology. In terms of mental health, for example, science currently asserts the effectiveness of cognitive behavioral therapy for mental health and wholeness, while scripture declares that "in Christ" one can be transformed into a new creation. Further, Romans 12:1 indicates that we are transformed by renewing our mind with the Word of God. The boundary or contact between the two is wholeness and cognition with both fields claiming a version of transformation through a change in the mind, cognitive restructuring and *metanoia* respectively. Although there are methodological parallels, the distinctions are clear as well. There is cognitive-behavioral theory on the one hand and soteriology on the other. The former is empirically derived from observing cognitive functions and processes and their relation to emotions and behaviors, while the latter is theological truth derived from revelation in scripture. The agent of change in the former is the client who has been equipped with proper CBT (cognitive-behavioral therapy) techniques, while the agent of change in the latter is the Holy Spirit who alone can transform a sinner into a regenerated child of God.

Can these two approaches effectively work together without conflation or reduction? I was appointed as an urban pastor to a low-income inner-city context where health insurance coverage and the median income were well below the national average. Many that attended our church were in recovery and struggling with mental health issues that were underdiagnosed and undertreated. The challenge was to devise a wholistic, mental health strategy that was accessible, affordable, and effective to serve my community. An immediate historical precedent came to mind. In my own Methodist tradition, the case and ministry of John Wesley, the movement's founder, stood out. Wesley's context within eighteenth-century England at the height of industrialization and urbanization was inundated with social ills, such as the slave trade, child labor, extreme class distinction, unemployment, overcrowded and unsanitary urban living conditions, debilitating poverty, malnutrition, lack of clean water, rampant alcoholism, and the list goes on. As early Methodists ministered to the souls of the masses, they encountered the physical and social struggles of the poor and working class, including inadequate health care. Wesley seemed to take an integrative approach to the problem, incorporating the science of his day with practical theology and ministry, specifically, a ministry of wholistic healing that incorporated a stout soteriology with the latest scientific and medical research of his day. Though clearly a revivalist invested in the spiritual well being of lives, he also knew the social implications of ministering the gospel and was equally invested in the overall well being and living conditions of those that early Methodism touched. Wesley's robust soteriology was driven by a quest for both spiritual and physical wholeness, and he employed whatever means were available to attain it. Wesley understood salvation as restorative and curative in nature and combined a variety of resources that were accessible to him at that time to minister to both soul and body of early Methodists.

Wesley recognized both spiritual and natural factors that cause health problems, as well as spiritual and natural factors that treat health problems. Rarely, did Wesley take a single approach, but often integrated a variety of treatments that were available, including prayer, medicine, herbs roots and other natural medicine, rest, exercise, diet, electricity, and other remedies.[33] Wesley's integrative approach, I suspect, was probably rooted in his understanding of prevenient grace in creation. God's prevenient grace and goodness are bestowed upon all flesh. For Wesley, all of nature is in a state of grace. Wesley was convinced that "there is no man that is in a state of mere nature; there is no man, unless, he has quenched the Spirit, that is wholly void of the grace of God."[34] Basic provisions should be available to all through every measure, including healing through the means of grace, medical science, and natural sources, such as proper diet and exercise.

Wesley's England experienced a shortage of medical practitioners as well as poor quality and unaffordable health care. In an effort to provide accessible, affordable, and efficient means that would address the health conditions of early Methodists, Wesley administered a vast array of treatments to attend to the people's needs along with the standard Methodist regimen of spiritual disciplines and means of grace found in their General Rules. He opened free clinics in London and Bristol and pharmaceutical dispensaries in London, Bristol, and Newcastle. In 1747 he published a *Primitive Physic: An Easy and Natural Method of Curing Most Diseases*, a book of available natural remedies for most ailments collected from Wesley's extensive research in the medical field of his day while some were handed down as folk medicine.[35] In the editions after 1772 Wesley marked an asterisk by his preferred

---

33. See Maddox, "John Wesley on Holistic Health and Healing," 4–33.

34. Wesley, "Working Out Our Own Salvation," 3:207.

35. *The Primitive Physic*, Wesley's most circulated work being published in 32 editions, was a collection of both natural, handed-down, folk remedies (nearly 1000) coupled with the latest medical treatments of Wesley's day, the former at times being a mixed bag of quackery and seemingly time-tested cures that Wesley claimed were tested and tried true.

remedies and "tried" by those he found to be effective.[36] He also made readily available and administered an early version of electrotherapy at his home and in Methodist free clinics through a portable and affordable "electrical machine," as described in his publication *The Desideratum, or, Electricity Made Plain and Useful*. A harmless, low voltage current was generated through friction by cranking the machine's handle and was used to shock the recipient. Wesley procured his electrical machine in 1756, while Franklin performed his famous experiment to attract lightning in 1752. The proximity of these events may suggest both that Wesley was privy to and versed in the latest scientific advances and that his use of electricity was highly experimental and may not always have yielded any helpful results, though he personally claimed a high rate of success on a few dozen different ailments.[37]

Wesley meticulously attended to every dimension of health and wholeness found in the eighteenth century. For physical strength and stamina, Wesley advocated for daily exercise for Methodists and specifically recommended walking and horseback riding for his preachers. If preachers could not get outside due to sickness, he encouraged them to obtain and ride an indoor chamber horse to accomplish the same purpose. Likewise, he prescribed a healthy regimen for the diet of his preachers, including plenty of water.[38] Wesley also witnessed divine healing and many miracles as well among early Methodists.[39] Functioning as a spiritual father to the emerging revival, Wesley assumed a wide range of care for early Methodists combining spiritual, natural, and medical treatments for health and wholeness.[40]Indeed, Wesley made a

36. Wesley, *Primitive*, vii.

37. Tyerman, *Life and Times of Rev. John Wesley, M.A.*, 162.

38. Wesley, *Primitive*, vii.

39. See Webster, *Methodism and the Miraculous*.

40. See the following secondary sources that address John Wesley, health and healing: Deborah Madden, Inward and Outward Health: John Wesley's Holistic Concept of Medical Science, the Environment and Holy Living (Eugene, OR: Wipf and Stock, 2012); Deborah Madden, "A Cheap, Safe, and Natural Medicine. Religion, Medicine, and Culture in John Wesley's Primitive Physic," Clio Medica 83, the Wellcome Series in the History of Medicine,

significant impact on eighteenth-century England, and we are easily tempted to romanticize Wesley's evangelistic work in general and specifically in regards to health care, highlighting its successes and minimizing its glitches and even failures. Although he was assisted by an apothecary and an experienced surgeon and claimed to refer acute and complicated cases to qualified physicians, under our standards of certification, he technically *practiced* medicine without a license. However, it is worth mentioning that Anglican clergy at that time were required to study basic medicine as part of their overall training.[41] Nonetheless, in his journals he recorded tremendous success, and in one entry he claims to have treated three hundred persons in three weeks, "many who had been ill for months or years were restored to "perfect health."[42] Wesley serves as a model for practicing an integrative approach to healing and wholeness.

TRUTH THERAPY AND DELIVERANCE

There are a host of examples before Wesley and since Wesley that have attempted to integrate science and theology.[43] I cite the amazing work of Global Awakening over the last two decades under its founder and overseer Randy Clark. This ministry, which has

2007; Deborah Madden, "Wesley as Adviser on Health and Healing" in The Cambridge Companion to John Wesley, eds Randy L. Maddox and Jason E. Vickers (Cambridge: Cambridge University Press, 2009), 176–89. Randy L. Maddox, "John Wesley on Holistic Health and Healing," Methodist History 46, no.1 (October 2007): 4–33.

41. Ibid.

42. *Works of John Wesley,* ed. Jackson, *Journals,* volume 2, reprinted (Kansas City: Beacon Hills Press, 1986), 39. Wesley does record cases where remedies did not obtain the desired result. And at times when administering the electrical machine he would qualify that 'none were harmed.' However, accounts of any blatant malpractice cases are difficult to find in his journals.

43. Some scientists, such as Francis Collins, John Polkinghorne, Arthur Peacocke, Malcolm Jeeves, Andrew Newberg, Matthew Stafford, and others including the work of BioLogos engage in interdisciplinary work within the areas of neuroscience, psychology and theology. Much of their work has contributed to an integrative approach to mental health and wholeness.

touched lives on every continent across the globe, has seen miraculous cases of healing and deliverance, even persons raised from the dead. Clark has been meticulous to work with medical professionals to not only approach healing wholistically but also to seek documentation and corroboration of his ministry's healing from an array of medical professionals across a variety of fields. To this end Clark has helped establish an outside organization in concert with medical professionals and scholars from various fields entitled GMRI, the Global Medical Research Institute (globalmri. org), a 501(c)(3) for the very purpose of bringing rigorous scrutiny and medical examination to claims of healing, deliverance, and miracles in Christian ministry. Work such as that of GMRI is not only advancing the credibility of Christian healing and deliverance ministries, but it is also advancing integrity in the interdisciplinary work between the fields of theology and science.

Like Wesley and later Randy Clark, I felt the need to integrate my faith with the work of the sciences to better serve God's people. As a pastor in an impoverished urban community where resources were limited, I found myself in a similar situation where it became necessary and most beneficial to be creative and draw from a variety of sources. As I began my work, the statistics and my suspicions were soon confirmed that many in the inner city could not afford health care, especially mental health care. Many of the persons that our church and recovery ministry had touched were experiencing mental disorders, including depression and anxiety. Some of those persons professed faith in Christ and others did not. In either case, very few were diagnosed or treated for their illness. Some could not afford treatment. Others believed that their Christian faith was sufficient for healing, while others were in denial about their condition. In order to minister in this demanding context, our congregation was intentional about constructing a comprehensive healing ministry that would be wholistically incorporating the healing graces that could be found through a variety of sources.

Our men's group built an exercise facility in the basement of the church, fully outfitted with both low and high impact

ient for both women and men. Fitness classes of all sorts
fered in the facility along with regular hours of operation
for walk-ins. I also taught a course on intentional diaphragmatic
breathing in concert with mindful prayer in the Hesychastic tradition to aid in the relief of stress, depression, and anxiety.[44] In
terms of diet and nutrition, our church had a food pantry and soup
kitchen that ministered to the indigent in the community and at
times offered cooking and nutrition classes. Our church building
was sizeable with unused space some of which was rented out to
our county health department. They regularly offered health fairs,
free screening and immunization, as well as informational semi-
nars for the public.

Our leadership did its best to make referrals to medical professionals when needed and to investigate and assist in financial
options for the needy. In terms of spiritual treatment, our local
congregation was charismatic in its theology and practice and
incorporated anointing the sick and prayer. Many of our spiritually gifted leaders, including medical professionals, were trained
in healing and deliverance ministries that involved the practice of
laying on of hands for physical, emotional, and mental healing in
personal, small group, and worship service settings. Discipleship
groups and a well-organized care system provided the emotional
support that is integral to combatting mental disorders. Persons
in our congregation claimed that it observed and confirmed many
miraculous healings, mostly physical but some mental. Yet, a small
percentage still suffered from mental disorders despite prayer and,
at times, despite professional therapy and even the use of SSRIs,
(selective serotonin reuptake, inhibitors) and other classes of anti-
depressants, and anti-anxiety meds.

One of the ways we addressed the concern of treatment-
resistant congregants, congregants that could not afford health
care, and a growing recovery constituency in our local church was
through one to one and small group support in discipleship. The

---

44. Hesychasm is a form of contemplative prayer in the Eastern Orthodox
tradition that involves breathing in rhythm with prayer usually with the Jesus
Prayer, "Lord Jesus Christ, Son of God, have mercy on me a sinner."

strategies and methods used in small group discipleship are not a substitute for medication or therapy, but function as a source of encouragement and a source for inner healing, spiritual formation, and direction. For those who were receiving treatment through medication and/or therapy, discipleship support functioned as a supplement. For those that could not afford health care, a small group was their sole support.

As these ministerial situations began to mount, I started to research more extensively cognitive behavioral therapy (CBT). I observed that although discipleship and CBT were two different practices operating out of two different frameworks, theology and psychology, the two were not mutually exclusive but had mutual points of contacts and shared a similar goal, which was functional wholeness. I discovered that the two could work compatibly as complements to service healthy belief formation, without reducing or conflating the two practices. I began to develop a model that integrated belief and identity formation and inner healing with cognitive behavioral theory and called it simply "truth therapy" and published it as a workbook out of our local church for our congregation and later for the public.

The term "therapy" is not used in a professional or clinical sense but draws from the eastern Christian notion of sin as soul sickness and salvation (*sozo*) as *therapeuo* or healing. The use of the word "truth" points to a cognitive approach, both from the basic principles of CBT and scripture's multiple injunctions that call for *metanoia* (repentance) and renewing the mind with the Word of God. The lies we believe bind us, but the truth sets us free. The lies we believe about God, ourselves, others, our past, and the world bind us. However, the truth we believe about these areas sets us free. Truth Therapy equipped persons to identify the lies that they believed and enslaved them and to repent and renounce them. Following, they would receive the truth found in scripture concerning each of these problematic areas. Renewing their minds with the truth would bring inner healing and even deliverance, as they learned who God really is and that they are a new creation in Christ. They discovered who God says that they are, and what

God says that they can do and possess. Persons experienced inner healing and were set free from the chains of the past trauma, addiction, or sin.

The *Truth Therapy*[45] model was developed from assimilating my research and work in discipleship, inner healing, and belief and identity formation with cognitive behavioral theory. The model started to emerge when asked, "Could cognitive behavioral theory assist Christian belief formation and further the spiritual formation needed for effective discipleship?" "Can scriptural teaching on renewing the mind with the Word of God work alongside CBT?" "Also could it assist parishioners who are struggling with anxiety and depression?" CBT (cognitive behavioral therapy), the most extensively used empirically based practice for mental health, equips clients with both an auto-didactic pedagogy to learn to identify cognitive distortion and related maladaptive behavior and also practical strategies, coping mechanisms, and techniques to unlearn distorted ideation and to restructure one's cognitive life in ways that are more realistic, objective, and flexible.[46]

CBT enables persons to test the validity of their own ideation, identify cognitive distortions, and then correct such distortions with realistic, hope-filled thinking that in turn generates a healthy emotional life and productive, desired behavior. Although I am not a licensed therapist and never claimed to be or operate as one, I realized that the methodology of CBT could be applied to belief formation and practices such as repentance and faith and other classical spiritual disciplines that are instrumental to formation. I learned to incorporate CBT practices, such as empirical questioning of beliefs into contemplative self-examination, self-correcting

45. Bellini, *Truth Therapy*.

46. CBT continues to be tested and modified for effectiveness. Mindfulness and Computerized Cognitive Behavioral Therapy are two popular ways in which this is occurring. Mindfulness is a significant component that has been added to the practice of CBT. With mindfulness CBT not only addresses the nature of the thoughts we think but also our relationship with our thinking. Awareness and reflection are thought to be resourceful tools that undergird the entire process and goal of CBT fostering clarity, flexibility, discipline, and objectivity in thinking.

ideation into repentance and cognitive affirmations into proper belief formation. Basically, the psychological principles of CBT were embedded into a theological discipleship strategy for the purpose of spiritual formation.

Further research in neuroscience and neuroplasticity added a neurophysiological dimension and further confirmation of the model's hypothesis that truth-based thinking can contribute to mental health. Healthy thinking not only empirically impacts and shapes healthy emotions, but it also impacts and shapes neural networks and neurochemistry, as neuroscience is in the early stages of demonstrating the neural correlates to CBT's impact on cognition and emotions. I hypothesized that CBT and an integrative approach such as *Truth Therapy* could function as self-directed neuroplasticity that shapes the brain for higher adaptability and the mind for healthier mental and emotional life.[47] Of course, much work and testing need to be done to determine the connections between CBT and neuroscience and neuroplasticity, and with the larger connection between brain and mind.[48]Although the *Truth Therapy* model affirms and incorporates CBT, it does not signify that this type of therapy is the solution, the only solution, or the best solution and that there are no problems with it. There is an increasing body of literature available that is critiquing CBT and countering its claims to effective treatment of mental disorders and claiming a declining effectiveness with the treatment.[49] I have

47. There are similar works like *Truth Therapy* that integrate Christian theology with CBT. See Michelle Pearce, *Cognitive Behavioral Therapy for Christians with Depression: A Practical Tool Based Primer*. Michael Free, *CBT and Christianity: Strategies and Resources for Reconciling Faith and Therapy*.

48. The problem of the brain-mind connection is augmented when one factors in notions of the soul or spirit or any immaterial aspect of human being. Much work is being done in version of the quantum brain to find a correlation between quantum mechanics and neuroscience that would allow for human factors and variables such as consciousness, freedom, intentionality will and others that in turn would serve as defeaters for a materialist or reductive anthropology. For a thorough treatment of the integration of CBT and neuroscience, see Nataša Jokić-Begić, "Cognitive-Behavioral Therapy and Neuroscience: Towards Closer Integration," 235–54.

49. See Laws and McKenna, "Cognitive behavioral therapy for major

an uneducated hunch that this may be a plateauing effect of the rapidly growing success of CBT. The future of CBT remains to be seen, though the Word of God abides forever.

Over time what did become more and more clear in ministry was that much of the healing work my co-workers and I attempted solely through deliverance proved less effective than the healing work that integrated multiple disciplines, including the mental health profession along side, Truth Therapy (discipleship with CBT principles) with deliverance as a last resort when needed. We achieved better results when we evaluated on a case by case and relied on an integrated approach that involved discipleship, the medical field and other wholistic treatment specifically suited for each unique situation. When deliverance was ministered, it was in concert with other types of care, primarily discipleship and inner healing, and as a last resort, which signified that we ruled out other causes that could be treated by other means.

Although a majority of the personal narratives from our local church and other churches that were practicing the model seemed to experience vast improvements in Christian growth and mental health, as confirmed by medical professionals, family, and colleagues, there are no easy answers or solutions, and the solutions at best assist in coping and thriving on the pathway of healing until more effective treatment is made available with the advances in medical science. Theologians, pastors, and laity can address this issue best by researching and incorporating the ongoing effective and compassionate work from the medical field as well as from other relevant disciplines.

Additionally, we need to examine in general the claims of science as well as the claims of theology and weigh them out critically by cross-examining claims with other theories, evidence, and cases that confirm, contradict, or support in part such claims and then modify our theories. Postmodern hermeneutics guide

---

psychiatric disorder: does it really work? A meta-analytical review of well-controlled trials," 9–24 and Johnsen and Friborg, "The effects of cognitive behavioral therapy as an anti-depressive treatment is falling: A meta-analysis," 747–68.

us to be aware constantly of the ideologies and agendas that lie underneath our research projects and our conclusions and that often direct them.[50] Political, social, and moral constructs, ideologies, and agendas at times are used to drive and shape scientific research., including a biomedical model of mental health. Also, it is imperative to keep updated on the rigorous pace of information that is generated within a particular field, especially mental health. It is not uncommon for this year's claims to be obsolete next year. Continuing education is part of what is necessary for a balanced approach to mental health and deliverance. This instrument is an attempt at such an integrated model of healing.

50. Foucault, *Madness and Civilization*.

6

Introduction to this Instrument

> "But if I drive out demons by the finger of God, then the
> kingdom of God has come upon you."—Luke 11:20

WHEN DOES SOMEONE NEED deliverance? The C1-13 probability
assessment is a qualitative and quantitative research instrument
that evaluates the probability of the need for deliverance. The
C1-13 measures the degree of bondage to a sinful practice and
evaluates the need for deliverance with a score that will indicate
whether deliverance is needed or not needed. This instrument
seeks to identify areas of bondage and to ascertain the degree of
bondage in a given area with the understanding that to the degree
one submits to an area or practice to that degree the sinful practice
has authority or control over one's will. This proportional relationship between submission and control, as mentioned above, is the
law of (will and) authority. One of the main goals in deliverance is
the liberation of the will, and the goal is attained by taking authority in the name of Jesus over the powers that hold one's will in
captivity, resulting in a will that is liberated to believe in Christ and
choose righteousness. Satan may tempt us, but we have the choice
to resist him, and he will flee (James 4:7).

The overall C1-13 instrument is broken up into five main
sections. The sections are *Personal Information, Inventory of Prior
Treatment of the Problem, Ten Point Checklist, the Assessment*

How the forms is set up

Inventory, and the *Score Sheet.* The first three sections are in-tended to gather information to acquire a comprehensive picture of the problem and document prior treatment, especially from other fields such as psychiatric treatment, clinical therapy, pastoral counseling, or even small group accountability. The premise is that a deliverance session is the last resort to alleviating symptoms and solving the problem. Other normative spiritual measures and normative healthcare need to be considered wholistically and prior to a deliverance session. These first three sections assist in locating holes or missing pieces in a comprehensive plan of treatment and refer clients to attend to such areas prior to participating in a deliverance session. If one has any items marked (F) FALSE on the Ten Point Checklist, they are to address those prior to continuing with the deliverance assessment process.

The final two sections of the C1-13 instrument are the actual assessment inventory and the score sheet, which is a worksheet for tallying up the composite score and evaluating the score for the need for deliverance. The assessment inventory is divided into *eight categories* or classes of sinful practices with an itemized list of practices under each category. The eight categories of sinful practices are *occult, mental health-related, addictive, sexual, criminal, religious, family of origin, and other.* The person taking the assessment marks each practice that they or a family member is involved. Family member involvement impacts all members and can open the door to the demonic for the entire family, and hence it must be identified. The assessment scores each practice in relationship to four variables: *generations, frequency, duration,* and *intensity of practice.* From these four scores a composite score (BQ—Bondage Quotient) is derived. The BQ score is then evaluated in terms of the probable need for deliverance.

There are two notable distinctions made in this instrument. The first is that mental disorders are not demonic in themselves. The second is that deliverance is different from exorcism. First, it is important to recognize that mental disorders are not demonic in themselves, but they can impair the person in a way that can open the door to demonic attack and demonization. There is an awareness inventory under section two of the assessment that helps the client identify current mental health issues that may render one susceptible to certain sinful and demonic practices. This inventory does not contribute to the actual scoring of demonization but is used for critical self-awareness. Following this awareness inventory is an actual inventory of related sinful practices that are to be scored.

When deemed necessary proper, psychiatric treatment and counseling must precede any assessment of deliverance. Often many confuse mental disorder for the demonic. I have watched too many persons unsuccessfully try to cast out schizophrenia, rather than treat the disorder, minister inner healing, and then cast out spirits (if there are any) that attacked the individual due to the disorder. Once mental healthcare professionals properly treat the mental disorder, it often becomes clearer what is a clinical issue and what is a demonic issue. If a mental health issue is detected and treatment has not been prescribed yet, then refer to a mental health professional. Second, it is also significant to note that this assessment makes a distinction between deliverance and exorcism. The former involves degrees of demonic influence and can even occur in believers. The latter is rare and involves demonic possession and cannot occur in believers. The former involves degrees of demonization and control, while the latter involves total demonization and control.

Although this instrument seeks to assess areas and degrees of demonization, again, not every Christian challenge or trial involves a direct encounter with a demon or needs intercessory deliverance. As referenced above, the normative way to deal with sin and evil is through resisting temptation, sin, and the devil with the power God gives us. The Lord has thoroughly equipped the church with a variety of weapons for the battle. For instance, God gives us power in his name, Scripture, his armor, his blood, the cross, and his presence to do battle with sin and evil. In our everyday struggles with evil, we are called to take up our cross daily and put to death our flesh and its passions and temptations, Galatians 5:24.

As referenced throughout this work, the cross is our basis for deliverance. Romans chapter six distinctly reveals the power of the cross. The cross is God's method to crush sin and Satan. The power of sin, the devil, and death is destroyed at the cross. When Jesus died, we died. When Jesus was buried, we were buried. When Jesus resurrected, we resurrected. When Jesus ascended, we ascended. When we yield to the power of the cross, we experience that our old life is crucified and we are raised to new life in Christ and seated in a position of authority in heavenly places with Christ. From this position of authority, we are called to deny ourselves, take up our cross daily, follow Christ, and reckon ourselves dead unto sin and alive unto God. We are called to submit our lives as instruments of holiness and no longer as instruments of disobedience. This way of the cross (*via crucis*) is the normative scriptural method to deal with sin and the power of evil.

There are occasions however when we fall. If anyone does sin, we have an advocate, Jesus Christ. We are called to come to the throne of mercy and confess and repent of our sins. If we turn from our sin and turn towards God, God will forgive us of our sin, and the blood of Jesus Christ cleanses us from all unrighteousness (1 Jn. 1:7-9). Yet, there are instances even following sin and repentance that one cannot break the cycle because a door to the demonic has been opened. In other cases, one continues in a sin(s), opens the door to the demonic, is oppressed and needs assistance through the ministry of deliverance in order to be liberated.

When ministering deliverance it is important that deliverance is ministered by church leadership that has been trained, certified, and recognized in this area. Deliverance needs to be ministered in teams of two or more. Also, there needs to be pre and post work that contributes to the overall deliverance process.[1] The pre and post work involves teaching, counseling, repentance, confession, faith and forgiveness, inner healing, renewing the mind with the Word of God, accountability, prayer and discipleship. It is also

---

1. I recommend much of the inner healing and deliverance work by John Loren Sandford. Also see Peter Bellini. *Truth Therapy*, Wipf and Stock, 2014 for needed follow-up work in belief and identity formation.

essential to approach deliverance and healing wholistically. Utilize all of the necessary means and treatment available that can work together comprehensively. For example, spiritual disciplines,[2] the means of grace,[3] proper diet, goal related exercise, intentional diaphragmatic deep breathing, good sleep habits, counseling, and medication when needed can work well together with prayer to minister healing to persons struggling with depression and anxiety. If persons are on medication do not counsel persons to stop treatment. Let all doctor prescribed treatment be assessed by the doctor alone. Leave medical counsel, diagnosis and prescribing to the medical professionals. Whether the case is related to a mental disorder or even demonic influence, the minister needs to take seriously the first Methodist General rule and so-called Hippocratic Oath and maxim, *primum non nocere* (First, to do no harm). Non-maleficence, "First, do no harm," is wisdom that one should proceed with caution and consider the soundness, risk, and consequences of any action, intervention or treatment. One needs to even consider if the intended course of treatment may make matters worse. Hence, when in doubt consider referral to one who is a professional or more experienced in addressing the problem.[4]

2. Foster, *Celebration of Discipline.*

3. John Wesley identified the following as means of grace in the "Nature, Design, and General Rules of Our United Societies:" attending the public worship of God, the ministry of the Word, the Lord's Supper, family and private prayer, searching the scriptures, and fasting or abstinence as well as attending small group meetings for prayer and accountability.

4. Critiques of the so-called Hippocratic Oath are common and are directed at its alleged impracticality in real situations within medical practice. Taken to an extreme, "doing no harm," would neutralize physicians from most treatment due to minor risks, side effects, and uncertainties. For example see https://www.health.harvard.edu/blog/first-do-no-harm-201510138421.

7

The C1-13 Integrative Deliverance Needs Assessment

Can be filled out by the client, minister, or deliverance team leader in an interview

PERSONAL INFORMATION

NAME _____

ADDRESS _____

PH # _____ **SEX** ( ) M ( ) F **AGE** _____

MARITAL STATUS: ( )Single ( )Married ( )Divorced
( )Remarried ( )Widowed

PROFESSION _____

( )Single ( ) Married ( )Divorced ( )Divorced and Remarried
( )Widowed

YOUR PARENTS' STATUS _____

NUMBER OF CHILDREN AND AGES _____

CURRENTLY IN COUNSELING ( ) Y N ( )For how long? _____

CURRENTLY TAKING MEDS ( ) Y N ( ) Names of meds_____

HOW LONG ON MEDS? _____

HOW MANY HOURS OF SLEEP DO YOU GET A NIGHT ?_____

**HAVE YOU GAINED OR LOST MORE THAN FIVE POUNDS IN THE
LAST MONTH?** Yes ( ) No ( )

HAVE YOU EXPERIENCED LOSS OF APPETITE OR INCREASED APPETITE LATELY? Yes ( ) No ( )

DO YOU HAVE CONSTIPATION OR DIARRHEA IN THE LAST MONTH?
Yes ( ) No ( )

HAVE YOU EXPERIENCED LATELY LOSS OF INTEREST IN THINGS YOU ONCE ENJOYED? Yes ( ) No ( )

HAVE YOU EXPERIENCED ANY OF THE FOLLOWING: a strange invisible presence? ( ), hearing voices in your head ( ), strange sights or sounds in your house ( ), thoughts that someone or something is watching you ( ), moments of blanking or blacking out.

Have you had odd experiences lately, such as nightmares ( ), accidents ( ), sudden significant financial loss ( ), irregular fights with family members ( ), explosive fits or rage ( ), other _____?

Any other mental health issues in your family, past or present?_____

FAITH INFORMATION

DO YOU CURRENTLY ATTEND A LOCAL CHURCH? ( ) Y ( ) N
NAME_____

HOW LONG ATTENDED? _____

DO YOU PROFESS SAVING FAITH IN JESUS CHRIST? ( ) Y ( ) N
DATE OF SALVATION _____

HAVE YOU BEEN BAPTIZED IN THE HOLY SPIRIT? ( ) Y ( ) N
DATE _____

ARE YOU FAMILIAR WITH PHENOMENA SUCH AS THE WORK OF THE SPIRIT, ANGELS AND EVEN DEMONS? ( ) Y ( ) N

DO YOU HAVE A TIME OF REGULAR PRAYER AND BIBLE STUDY?
( ) Y ( ) N **HOW MUCH TIME?** _____

ARE YOU INVOLVED IN ANY MINISTRY? _____

FOR HOW LONG? _____

REASON FOR THIS DELIVERANCE APPOINTMENT

DESCRIPTION OF PROBLEM AND SYMPTOMS _____

_____

_____

_____

_____

IS THERE A FAMILY HISTORY OF THIS PROBLEM?
( ) Y ( ) N Explain_____

INVENTORY OF PRIOR TREATMENT OF THE PROBLEM

Since deliverance is a means and a subset of healing, it is often helpful to think of deliverance in terms of wholeness and health. Issues of health are often treated wholistically and comprehensively from an integrated approach that affords the best resources from faith and science. Thus, it can be helpful and effective to approach certain problems and issues with multiple types of treatment that impact body, mind, emotions and spirit. Indicate which types of treatment you have used or are currently using.

WHAT OTHER FORMS OF TREATMENT FOR THE PROBLEM HAVE YOU USED? MARK (X) AND FILL IN BLANKS.

____**Repentance**. What type _____How long _____
         Results _____

____**Medical**. What type _____How long ___
         Results _____

____**Counseling**. What type _____How long _____
         Results_____

____**Support Group**. What type _____How long _____
         Results_____

____**Prison or Jail**. What type _____How long _____
         Results_____

___**Medication**. What type _____How long _____
        Results_____

___**Prayer group**. What type _____How long _____
        Results_____

___**Prior Deliverance**. What type _____How long _____
        Results_____

___**Confession and forgiveness**. What type_____How long___
        Results_____

___**Diet**. What type _____How long _____
        Results_____

___**Exercise**. What type _____How long _____
        Results _____

___**Sleep therapy**. What type _____How long ___
        Results _____

OTHER LIFESTYLE CHANGES.

What type _____How long _____
Results _____
Other _____

TEN POINT CHECKLIST

Mark (T) for each statement that is TRUE. Mark (F) for each statement that is FALSE. Any item marked (F) FALSE needs to be addressed with the proper professional, (general physician, psychiatrist, therapist, or pastor) before continuing with the inventory assessment. Note, you cannot continue with the assessment if you have marked (F) FALSE on any of the ten statements. Stop and address each item first as instructed in the FOLLOW-UP section before continuing. Answer the following statements either (T) or (F):

1.   Confessing sin, repentance and faith, forgiveness, accountability, and participation in worship, inner healing prayer,

and discipleship groups are not breaking the cycles of sin or oppression in an area. ( )

2. Attempts at prayer, fasting and spiritual warfare and those by other intercessors are not breaking the cycles of sin or oppression in the area. ( )

3. You addressed your beliefs and practices, especially questionable ones, with your pastor or spiritual leadership in your church ( )?

4. Leadership discerns demonic presence and influence in your life ( )

5. You sense demonic influence in your life ( )

6. You visited a therapist or other mental health professionals for evaluation( )

7. Treatment such as counseling, medication, diet, exercise, rehabilitation, recovery group, or other form of treatment is not working ( )

8. You feel helpless in one or more area and struggle at times to perform daily functions. ( )

9. You have been seen by professionals (medical, pastoral, or other) about your problem(s) ( )

10. After trying other means of help, deliverance is seen as a last resort. ( )

FOLLOW-UP

Identify each numbered question that you responded (F) FALSE. Find that number below for follow-up instructions. For example if you responded FALSE to numbers six and nine, then go to numbers six and nine below and follow the instructions for each. After you have followed through with the instructions on each question answered FALSE, then you can proceed.

1. You need repentance and faith in that area of sin. Take time to follow up in this area. Participate in spiritual disciplines, the means of grace, confession of sin, repentance and faith, forgiveness, accountability with one or more persons, worship service, inner healing, or a discipleship group.

2. You may need to pray, fast, and execute spiritual warfare, as well as approach intercessors on your behalf to do the same. Take the time to follow up in this area.

3. Take time to meet with your pastor or spiritual leadership to address your specific beliefs and practices and have them evaluated by scripture, especially any questionable ones. Transformation of beliefs can lead to transformation of life and practice. Christian catechesis, conversion, and discipleship are all necessary for right belief, worship, and practice.

4. You need to make an appointment with leadership for prayer, discernment, and inner healing. Intercessors, prophets, spiritual directors, and counselors among other qualified leadership can assist you in hearing the voice of God and discerning God's direction and will for your life.

5. Take time to discern in prayer if you are battling an evil spirit(s).

6. Schedule an appointment with a therapist or other mental health professional to be evaluated concerning the problem.

7. Receive proper treatment from the proper professional (medical, mental health, social worker, sponsor, nutritionist, trainer etc.).

8. You may not need deliverance. Confide with a counselor, spiritual director, confidant, or accountability group or partner to make sure you are being open and honest about personal struggles in your life.

9. Discuss your problem with the proper professional including pastor, medical doctor, specialist, or mental health professional.

10. Have the problem addressed by all of the follow-up instructions given in 1-9.

If you marked (T) TRUE for all 10 statements then proceed to take the Inventory Assessment to determine the probability for deliverance. If you have marked (F) FALSE in any of the boxes you should not continue with the assessment. Those areas need professional follow up prior to proceeding further with this assessment. Do not take the Inventory Assessment until you have had those areas addressed by a medical professional, psychiatrist, therapist, pastor, or other appropriate professional. Only proceed with the Inventory Assessment after marking (T) TRUE on all ten statements.

THE INVENTORY ASSESSMENT

Inventory of Practices

There is no formula, metric, or scientific test to discern with absolute precision the presence of demonization. Detected demonization is a spiritual process. One can discern demonization from scripture, the Holy Spirit, and the fruit in one's life if deliverance is possibly needed. However, the spiritual process of discernment can be aided by a qualitative analysis of behavior as well as a cross-evaluation with other disciplines in the hard and soft sciences, such as general medical practice, psychiatry, or clinical therapy. This inventory is a tool that assists the spiritual discernment process by working in concert with other professional fields while analyzing behavior that is considered sinful and possibly demonic according to the Christian scriptures. The C1-13 assumes cooperation with other professional fields and as an ultimate resort assess the probability and need for deliverance based on practices or fruit and the frequency, duration, and intensity of the practice. The inventory identifies doors of evil influence that may require deliverance. Not all of the practices necessarily entail demonization. The scoring following the inventory along with the ten point checklist above can ascertain the probability of demonization.

Practices indicated in the inventory by an asterisk can be highly traumatic and open up doors to the demonic and may not need to occur frequently but at times just once. Scoring is determined by the experience of the one taking the assessment.

Check off any of the following influences or practices that involve you or your family:

Occult Practices

__Witchcraft of any form
__Curses—cursing or cursed
__History of inexplicable systemic accidents, tragedies, or misfortunes
__Ouija board
__Crystals, charms, amulet use
__Numerology
__Fortune telling
__Hypnotism—giver or receiver
__Tarot cards
__Kabbalah
__Trances
__Books, music, movies or other forms depicting the occult
__Freemasonry or secret societies
__Levitation
__ESP, telekinesis
__Alchemy (modern type involving magic)
__Mind Reading
__Automatic Writing
__Astrology, zodiac
__Séance
__Satanism*
__Wicca
__Vampirism

__Crystal ball use

__Table lifting or other telekinesis

__Black Magic or magic of any type

__Divination

__Astral Projection or out of body experiences

__Channeling

__Spirit guides or mediums

__Clairvoyance

__Sacrifices*

__Necrophilia

__Contacting the dead or use of mediums

__Palm read or reading. Palmistry.

__Reiki or other types of healing

__Covenants, vows, oaths, pacts to any spirit or deity

__Psychics

__Do you possess books, movies, music, or any objects that have been used for non-Christian religious purposes, like masks, idols, statues, fetish objects etc., or for any of the above purposes?

__Gnostic type practices

__Summoning spirits, demons, the dead, or any non-physical beings*

__Role-play games involving any of the above

__Music, books, movies, games, or any paraphernalia etc. that involves any of the above occult activity.

__Animal abuse

__Other occult practices_____

List not exhaustive. See Christian Scriptures.

Destructive Practices (related to mental disorders)

NOTE: *It is important to recognize that mental disorders are not demonic in themselves, but they can impair the person in a way that can open the door to demonic attack and demonization. When necessary, proper psychiatric treatment and counseling must precede any assessment of deliverance. Often many confuse mental disorder for the demonic. Once a mental disorder is properly treated by mental healthcare professionals, it often becomes clearer what is a clinical issue and what is a demonic issue. If a mental health issue is detected and treatment has not been prescribed yet, then refer to a mental health professional.*

Check the following mental health issues to determine the susceptibility to unwanted or destructive practices. These items are NOT part of identifying and scoring practices used to assess the probability of the need for deliverance. Checked items create an awareness of vulnerability to certain practices. This list identifies mental health issues that may or may not be collaterally related to practices that are in need of deliverance. Mental disorder themselves are not necessarily demonic in themselves.

Awareness Inventory of Mental Disorders and Susceptibility

__Minor Depression Diagnosis from a Professional

__Major Depression Diagnosis from a Professional

__DSM-5 on Major Depressive Disorder. If one has five of the following nine symptoms daily.

1. __Depressed mood or irritable most of the day, nearly every day, as indicated by either subjective report.(e.g., feels sad or empty) or observation made by others (e.g. appears tearful).

2. __Decreased interest or pleasure in most activities, most of each day

3. __Significant weight change (5 percent) or change in appetite

4. __Change in sleep: Insomnia or hypersomnia

5. __Change in activity: Psychomotor agitation or retardation

6. __Fatigue or loss of energy

7. __Guilt/worthlessness: Feelings of worthlessness or excessive or inappropriate guilt

8. __Concentration: diminished ability to think or concentrate, or more indecisiveness

9. __Suicidality: Thoughts of death or suicide, or has suicide plan

__Mood Disorder/Bipolar Diagnosis from a Professional
__Schizophrenia Diagnosis from a Professional
__Panic or Panic attacks
__Anxiety Disorder Diagnosis from a Professional
__DSM 5 - The presence of excessive anxiety and worry about a variety of topics, events, or activities. Worry occurs more often than not for at least six months, and is clearly excessive. The individual experiences at least three characteristic symptoms including:

1. __restlessness or feeling keyed up or on edge

2. __being easily fatigued; always tired

3. __difficulty concentrating or mind going blank; difficulty focusing

4. __irritability; easily disturbed

5. __muscle tension

6. __and sleep disturbance

__ADD Diagnosis from a Professional
__ADHD Diagnosis from a Professional
__OCD—Compulsions or compulsive behavior. Diagnosis from a Professional
__ODD (Oppositional, Defiant). Diagnosis from a Professional
__Hearing voices
__Trauma* (from any number of incidents of war, abuse, or other)
__Racing thoughts
__Very difficult to focus

Susceptible to Destructive Practices—These items are to be identified and scored to assess probability for the need of deliverance. Score the following items:

__Suicidal (ideation, plans, or attempts)

__Death wish (want to die)

__Self-mutilation or cutting

__Compulsions or compulsive behavior _____

_____

__Thoughts and feelings of rejection or low self esteem

__Hallucinations, irrational paranoia, or hearing voices not related to treated Schizophrenia. These symptoms should be first assessed by a mental health professional

__Feelings and thoughts of hopelessness, worthlessness, and helplessness

__Violent behavior towards self or others

__Lying or stealing

__Promiscuity

__Criminal behavior (See section #5)

__Vertigo, dizziness, or involuntary movement or manifestation not related to other somatic or mental health issues

__Night terrors/violent nightmares

__Fear (undifferentiated)

__Fear of people, crowds, death, opposite sex, the dark, future, sickness or disease, or any other specific type

__Obsession(s)

__Any addictive behaviors (See section #3)

__Other unwanted or destructive practice

Addictions/Addictive Practices

__Alcohol, drunkenness

__Prescription Drugs_____

__Illegal drugs _____

__Marijuana, Hashish, Opium.

__Heroin

__LSD, Hallucinogenics, N-Bombs
__Krokodil
__Methamphetamines. Crystal Meth.
__Opioids of any sort like Gray Death, Fentanyl, Pink AH-7921, and others.
__Flakka, bath salts.
__Ecstasy
__Molly
__Anabolic steroids
__Crack Cocaine, Cocaine.
__Pornography
__Cigarettes
__Sexual addictions
__Gambling
__Excessive, compulsive or needless spending or spending sprees
__Obsessive and compulsive Internet use
__Internet chatting, dating, sexting, or encounters for sexual or illicit purposes
__Other_____

List not exhaustive

Sexual Practices

__Any sexual practice forbidden in Scripture (See Bible)
__Autoeroticism
__Polyamorous relationships
__Pornography
__Adultery*
__Fornication*
__Lust
__Incest—victim* or perpetrator*
__Abuse of others*
__Experienced sexual abuse*
__Pedophilia*
__Prostitution

__Paraphilias

__Necrophilia

__SMBD

__Incubus, succubus, or sexual experience with a presence in dreams or awake at night

__Voyeurism, stripping or watching, or exhibitionism

__Bestiality*

__Rape* or raped*

__Molest* or molested*

__Perverse forms of sex or sexuality

__Confusion around one's gender or sex (may not be demonic itself but may invite demonic attack)

__Other_____

List not exhaustive. See Christian Scriptures.

Criminal Practices

__Theft, forcible entry,

__Murder*, homicide, manslaughter

__False witness, perjury

__Assault or battery of any kind

__Racketeering

__Extortion, conspiracy, or treason

__Manslaughter*

__Homicide*

__Gang affiliation

__Fraud _____

__Drug use, sales

__Prostitution

__Incarcerated

__Experienced physical, mental, verbal, or sexual abuse

__Sex trafficking/trafficked* or Work trafficking/trafficked*

__Other_____

List not exhaustive. See Christian Bible.

Religious Practices

Note: Religious affiliations do not always necessitate demonization and the need for deliverance. As a religious affiliation facilitates beliefs and practices contrary to scripture, it can open the door to sin that in turn can open the door to the demonic. However, it is significant to note that some religious affiliations teachings about the nature and activity of God or moral conduct may even parallel or be in line with the teaching of scripture and not be sinful or demonic. For example, a religion may teach that God created the universe, or that stealing, lying, and adultery are forbidden practices. Sinful practices and potential doors to the demonic are identified by Christian scripture. World and folk religions, even beliefs, practices, and forms claiming to be "Christian," new religious movements, cults[1], various spiritual movements that foster unbiblical beliefs and practices not only can be sinful but also can open the door to the demonic. These items are to be identified and scored to assess probability for the need of deliverance. *Score the following items:*

__Idolatry - Prayer, use of artifacts in magic or worship, communication, or a specific practice or devotion to any god besides the God of the Christian scriptures

__Doctrine of devils and seducing spirits: World religions, indigenous religions, or Christian syncretistic religions with unbiblical teachings and practices, for example Baha'ism, any polytheistic or animistic religions and others. Can include false doctrines held within a Christian denomination or by an individual unrelated to any movement.

---

1. According to sociologist William Bainbridge, "A cult movement is a deviant religious organization with novel beliefs and practices. William Sims Bainbridge, *The Sociology of Religious Movements*, 24. Due to pejorative examples and connotations of the word cult, this particular use of cult from derived from sociology and anthropology of religion is not in current use as much as "new religious movements." However, this instrument is claiming that both new religious movements and the more limited, pejorative use of cult need to be examined for beliefs and practices and weighed out culturally through critical contextualization in light of scripture.

__Cultic Manipulation, Control and Abuse found in "Christian" cults, such a Mormonism, Jehovah's Witnesses, Unification Church (the Moonies), Boston Movement, Christadelphians, Rosicrucian, or others.

__Cultic Manipulation, Control and Abuse found in non-Christian cults, such as Scientology, Eckankar, Twelve Tribes, EST (the Forum), the Family, NXIVM and others.

__Religions, syncretism, folk religions, or spirituality that uses sorcery, channeling, mediums, magic, fetishes, spells, enchanted objects, or any other means to conjure, communicate, contact, gain power, or be influenced by spirits or the spirit realm, such as New Age, paganism, Wicca, shamanism, Satanism, Freemasonry, secret societies, paganism, Course in Miracles, Umbanda, macumba, malocchio, distinu, Santeria, Yoruba, orichas, Voodoo or other similar forms and practices.

__Legalism of any sort whether Christian or non-Christian religion.

__Doctrines and practices of racism and racial supremacy regardless of race.

__Practices of witchcraft

__Book of Urantia

__Necromancy

__Trances

__Curses: given or received

__Conjuring spirits

__Spirit possession (intentional or unintentional)

__Talking to spirits

__Sacrifices

__Covenant or alliances made to any spirit or god besides the God of Christian scripture.

__See occult practices

__Ancestor worship (beyond honoring) that involves devotion as unto God or covenants and alliances made.

__Other

List is not exhaustive. See Christian Scriptures.

Family of Origin Practices

__Occult_____

__Addiction _____

__Sinful or destructive practices related to mental
disorder_____

__Criminal acts _____

__Unbiblical religious belief or practice_____

__Sexual Sin _____

__Divorce

__Abortion or survivor of one.

__Rejection issues, orphaned, abandoned. Other rejection issues.

__Trauma

__Prone to systemic accidents, injuries, sickness, miscarriage,
financial crises, premature death etc.

__Incest*

__Rebellion

__Disobedience to parents

__Abuse (sexual, physical, mental or verbal)

__Other _____

List not exhaustive. See Christian Scriptures

Other Sinful Practices

___Pride

___Jealousy

___Lust

___Laziness or sloth

___Envy

___Greed

___Gossip, slander, backbiting

___Condemnation

___Judging, judgmental

___Unforgiveness

___Hatred

____Spirit of fear or fear of future, others, opposite sex, heights, closed spaces, death, sin, insanity, water, going outside, and other objects of fear.

____Competition

____Rebellion

____Idolatry

____Anger or rage

____Swearing/cursing

____Drunkenness

____Gluttony

____Malice

____Blasphemy

____Profanity

____Taking God's name in vain

____Lying, false witness, deceit

____Heresy

____Division, schism

____Legalism

____Bitterness

____Experienced familial, marital, short or long-term abuse of any type

____Books, movies, games, music or other forms that depict sinful practices that have influenced your behavior

____Other _____

List not exhaustive. See Christian Scriptures

Evaluation of each practice:

Score each practice that was flagged in the inventory of practices by assigning a numerical value (1 to 5) to each of the four areas of assessment (generations, duration, frequency, and intensity). The total score represents the Bondage quotient. Note some practices need only occur once to open the door to the demonic and require deliverance.

The C1-13 Integrative Deliverance Needs Assessment

Generational Sin—Over how many generations has it been practiced?

1. First generation
2. Two generations
3. Three generations
4. Four generations
5. Five generations

Duration—How long has it been practiced?

1. Less than 3 months
2. 3 months to a year
3. At least a year
4. 1-5 years
5. More than 5 yrs.

Frequency—How frequently has it been practiced?

1. A few times a year.
2. Once a week to once a month
3. 3 times a week
4. Daily
5. More than 3 times a day

Intensity—How intensely has it been practiced?

1. Practice with little interest and passion
2. Practice with some interest and passion
3. Practice with moderate interest and passion.
4. Practice with high interest and passion
5. Practice with intense commitment and passion

SCORESHEET

Type of Practice.	Frequency	Intensity	Duration	Generational	BQ-Total

EVALUATION OF BQ COMPOSITE SCORE (THE BONDAGE QUOTIENT) FOR EACH PRACTICE

0—No Deliverance needed—0%

1-5—Need for repentance and faith with very low probable need for deliverance- 0-20%

6-10—Repentance and faith needed with low to moderate probable need for deliverance- 20-50%

11-15 - Need for deliverance is moderate to likely probable—50%-70%

16-20—Need for deliverance is highly probable—70%-100%

https://www.academia.edu/36993369/THE_C-13_INTEGRATIVE_
DELIVERANCE_NEEDS_ASSESSMENT

8

Legal Waiver for Ministry

LEGAL PROTECTION FROM LIABILITY when ministering deliverance is a wise consideration. Besides training workers in proper ministry conduct and boundaries that can prevent infractions of misconduct, harassment, abuse, and similar charges, ministries should have participants sign a release of liability. Here is a sample waiver drawn up by my lawyer. This sample can be used as a template or guide for crafting one specific to your own context. I recommend your ministry or local church draw up its own that is approved by its Board of Trustees and is based on the laws of your State and the specific context of your ministry.

RELEASE AND WAIVER OF LIABILITY

DISCLAIMER: THIS FORM DOES NOT CONSTITUE
LEGAL ADVICE. ANYONE USING THIS FORM SHOULD
DO SO ONLY WTH THE ADVICE OF THEIR OWN
LEGAL COUNSEL.

READ BEFORE SIGNING.

IMPORTANT. READ CAREFULLY. This document affects your legal rights. You, the "Participant", must sign it whether you are an adult or minor, if you are participating in "Activities" (generally referred to as "Deliverance Ministry") facilitated by [CHURCH use actual legal entity] ("Facilitator").

Your parent or legal guardian must sign it also if you are a minor Participant (under eighteen years of age.) The parent or guardian agrees to these terms individually and on behalf of the minor. Only a parent or legally appointed guardian may sign for a minor Participant. References in this agreement to "I" or "We" include all who sign below unless otherwise clearly indicated.

PARTICIPANT AGREEMENT

(Including Acknowledgement and assumption of Risks, Agreements of Release and Indemnity, and Additional Provisions)

In consideration of the opportunity to participate in activities offered by Facilitator,

I, _____ (Please print name)	the Participant (adult or minor), and,
_____, (Please print name)	the parent or legal guardian of a minor Participant, understand, acknowledge and agree as follows:

ACTIVITIES, HAZARDS AND RISKS

The various activities may include [LIST ACTIVITIES].

The hazards and risks (together referred to as "risks") associated with the various activities may include [LIST], as well as associated reasonably foreseeable risks.

Participant, and the parent or guardian of a minor Participant, acknowledge and understand that the description of the activities and risks described herein is not complete and that all activities, whether or not described, may be dangerous and may include risks which are inherent and cannot be reasonably avoided without changing the nature of the activity.

Facilitator has made no effort to determine, and accepts no responsibility for, medical, physical or other qualifications or the suitability of Participant, or other participants, for the activities. [MAY NEED TO CHANGE THIS IF YOU DO BACKGROUND CHECKS, ETC]

Participant, and the parent or guardian of a minor Participant, accepts full responsibility for determining Participant's medical, physical or other qualifications or suitability for participating in the activities.

Participant, and the parent or guardian of a minor Participant, HEREBY CERTIFIES that the Participant, and the parent or guardian of a minor Participant has personal health insurance. Insurance company is _____

_____.

Alcohol will, and other substances may, impair judgment and reduce a Participant's ability to effectively manage the various risks described herein, and are therefore strictly prohibited by Facilitator except for necessary prescribed or over the counter medications, and if applicable, approved by the Parent or legal guardian of a minor participant. **Failure to adhere to instructions, should they be provided, may result in serious injury or death**.

ACKNOWLEDGMENT AND ASSUMPTION OF RISKS

I, the Participant (adult or minor) and the parent or guardian of a minor Participant, understand the nature of the services of Facilitator and other associated activities which may occur, and their risks. I acknowledge and expressly assume all risks of the activities, whether or not described above, known or unknown, and inherent or otherwise. I take full responsibility for any injury or loss, including death, which I, or the minor child for whom I sign, may suffer, arising in whole or part out of such activities.

AGREEMENT OF RELEASE AND INDEMNIFICATION, AND ADDITIONAL PROVISIONS

If I am an adult participant, or the parent or guardian of a minor Participant, I agree, for myself and on behalf of the minor Participant for whom I am signing, as follows:

I release Facilitator, its employees, contractors, volunteers, and directors ("Released Parties") from any and all claims of injury or loss which I, or the minor child for whom I sign, may suffer arising out of or in any way related to my, or the minor's, enrollment in or participation in the activities of Facilitator. Neither I, the minor child, nor anyone acting on our behalf, will bring suit or otherwise assert any such claims against a Released Party. I will indemnify (that is, defend and satisfy by payment or reimbursement including costs and attorney's fees) each Released Party from any claim of liability, including one brought by or for a minor child whom I sign, a co-participant in any of the activities of Facilitator, a rescuer, a member of my, or the minor's family, or anyone else asserting a loss arising out of or on any way related to my, or the minor's enrollment in or participation in the activities of Facilitator.

ADDITIONAL PROVISIONS

I authorize Facilitator to provide or obtain for me, or the minor child for whom I sign such medical care as it considers necessary and appropriate, and I agree to pay all costs associated with such care and related transportation.

Any dispute between Facilitator and me or the minor child for whom I sign will be governed by the substantive laws of the

State of Ohio [VERIFY STATE] (not including the laws which might apply the laws of another jurisdiction).

This agreement is entered into voluntarily and after careful consideration. Its terms cannot be amended except in writing. I understand that it is binding, to the fullest extent allowed by law, upon all persons signing below, our respective heirs, executors, administrators, wards, minor children (whether or not they are Participants) and other family members.

If any part of this agreement is found by a court or other appropriate authority to be invalid, the remainder of the agreement nevertheless shall be in full force and effect.

I, and the minor child for whom I may sign for, read and understand the English language.

I or the minor child for whom I sign shall be responsible for the return of all equipment supplied by the Facilitator or independent contractor in the same condition that existed at the time of taking possession of said equipment and that no alcohol, intoxicating liquor or illegal drugs shall be taken or consumed during or in the course of any activity described herein.

Participant: _____ (Signature)	Age: ___	Date: ____
Parent or Legal Guardian: _____ (Signature)		Date: ____

9

Fifty Guidelines for Deliverance

NOTE: THERE IS NO strict formula or science to deliverance. Deliverance comes from the grace of God revealed in the finished work of Jesus Christ on the cross through the power of the Holy Spirit. Deliverance is Spirit-led and occurs through the faith of the believer, as he or she trusts in and implements the authority of the name of Jesus, given to them by Christ. Although there is no strict formula or magic phrase for deliverance, there are Biblical and Spirit-led wisdom and principles that can guide the process. Here are some guidelines and a general checklist of principles one can use:

1. After answering TRUE on all ten statements on the Ten Point Checklist, have the recipient fill out the release form. Remember not to administer deliverance if the person has not scored ten on the Checklist. ____

2. Assign the session to an available, well-trained, prepared and certified deliverance team (at least two-person, preferably three to four, mixed sexes) ____

3. It is good to have women take the lead with women and men with men ____

4. One should lay hands with permission, in only appropriate places, and on the same sex ____

5. Explain the process and ask permission at each juncture ____

6. Protect the dignity of the person above all ____

7. Be pastoral even over being prophetic ____

8. Deliverance team with designated leader is prayed and fasted up ____

9. Deliverance team has gone through a period of repentance and cleansing ____

10. Recipient has filled out inventory, waiver, and assessment form ____

11. Leadership has reviewed the results of the inventory and assessment with recipient ____

12. Leadership has interviewed recipient in terms of the problem, the inventory and assessment, the solution and deliverance procedures and expectations ____

13. Make sure deliverance team does not hinder the process in any way through improper dress, foul breath or odors, division, arguing, forcing of manifestations or the like ____

14. Set aside a special, private room for deliverance ____

15. Have the following items available—Bibles, bottles of water, power or granola bars or healthy snack items, towels, tissues, a garbage can, praise and worship music, breath fresheners, and other useful items ____

16. Saturate the room before, during and after deliverance with prayer, praise and worship____

17. Set aside an initial time for submission to God ____

18. Plead the blood of Jesus over the room, the team, and the recipient__

19. Invite recipient to repent of all sins and renounce all practices from both the inventory and whatever comes to their mind ____

20. Invite Jesus the Lion of the Tribe of Judah, the Dragon and Demon Slayer into the room to release deliverance ___

21. Ask for protection from warrior angels and release protection ___

22. Bind all distractions and hindrances ___

23. Ask permission from the person to lay on hands or for anything attempted ___

24. When necessary explain the process and its procedures to the candidate as you go along ___

25. Bind and break powers over the area and the deliverance team ___

26. Dismantle and deactivate all assignments and strategies of the enemy___

27. One person speaks at a time. Avoid confusion and distractions ___

28. Expect the Spirit to reveal the gifts of the Spirit, especially discernment, healing and words of knowledge and wisdom that will address names of spirits, types of afflictions, and strategies for victory ___

29. Do not allow demons to manifest or speak. They are liars___

30. Bind the strongman or ruling spirit and call it out by name if you know it ___

31. Address each spirit from the inventory or otherwise specifically by name and command it to come out in the name of Jesus ___

32. Break and renounce each of these spirits in Jesus' name ___

33. Curse the demonic powers with the blood of Jesus ___

34. Declare over the candidate repeatedly that Jesus is Lord; even insist that the demons acknowledge it as well ___

35. Remind Satan that all authority has been given to you in Jesus' name to bind him and cast him out ___

36. Throughout the session, as led by the Spirit, invite the candidate to repent of various sins and to renounce them, as well as to confess Jesus as Lord.

37. Only raise your voice if the Spirit leads, but it is not necessary for deliverance ____

38. Be led. Allow for others to speak and take the lead for a time ____

39. Be attentive to the person's dignity and honor. Do not hurt, harm, embarrass, or shame the person ____

40. Do not get physical in a way that can harm, hurt or violate the person. Be gentle but bold ____

41. Heaviness can harbor and manifest in the chest area. Pray over that area ____

42. Demons often nestle in the spirit that impacts the stomach area. Pray over that area ____

43. Do not struggle, wrestle or contest with demons unnecessarily or for prolonged periods. The person is either ready for deliverance, or they are not. The deliverance team knows their authority in Christ, or they do not ____

44. Continue to praise and worship Jesus throughout the session. Actually, Christ is the main focus during the deliverance session and not Satan ____

45. If the person is not willing to repent, renounce each spirit, or surrender to the point of breakthrough, do not force their will but discontinue the session for a latter date when the recipient is more open or ready ____

46. Close all open doors and seal them with the blood of Jesus ____

47. If the person has repented and is set free, invite the person to accept Christ as their Lord and Savior (if they have not already) and pray for the person to receive the infilling of the Holy Spirit where a vacancy has been created by the deliverance ____

48. Plead the blood for cleansing over all who have participated
___

49. Pray protection against backlash over each person and all
that pertains to the covenant in their lives ___

50. Schedule a follow-up session before leaving and begin
discipleship in *Truth Therapy* by Peter Bellini or a similar
work. Other recommended reading: *Deliverance and Inner
Healing*, John and Mark Sandford; *Christianity with Power*,
Charles Kraft; *The Bondage Breaker, Victory over the Dark-
ness, Who am I in Christ, Freedom From Addiction* and other
titles, Neil Anderson; *Deliverance from Evil Spirits*, Francis
MacNutt; *Biblical Guidebook to Deliverance*, Randy Clark;
How to Cast Out Demons, Doris Wagner; *Demons: the An-
swer Book*, Lester Sumrall; *Deliverance and Spiritual Warfare
Manual*, John Eckhardt; *Handbook for Spiritual Warfare*, Ed
Murphy among others.

Appendix

Affirmations of Faith

Post-delivery and recovery are essential to deliverance and wholeness. I recommend subsequent to deliverance that a person follows up with several items. Become a part of a small group for accountability and discipleship. Meet regularly with an accountability partner or sponsor. Seek a counselor or spiritual director to offer guidance and wisdom. Take an active part in one's own discipleship and formation. Find a mentor who will be willing to spend time in intentional discipleship. Begin to delve into discipleship material that will keep you on the road to recovery. Participate in all of the available means of grace, such as Bible study, prayer, worship services, Holy Communion, self-denial, fasting, giving, serving and other forms that communicate the grace of God.

Also as a part of post-deliverance and recovery, it is important for individuals to affirm their faith in the Father, the Lord Jesus Christ, and the Holy Spirit of historic Christianity. The Nicene Creed is a universally recognized symbol of faith accepted by most Christian communities. The creed was first hammered out at the First Council of Nicaea in 325 and amended at the First Council of Constantinople in 381. The Nicene Creed is generally accepted by the Christian church as the standard for orthodoxy. As the first step in post-deliverance recovery, let persons affirm their faith by reciting the Nicene Creed and meditating on its words.

THE NICENE CREED

We believe in one God,
   the Father, the Almighty,
   maker of heaven and earth,
   of all that is, seen and unseen.

We believe in one Lord, Jesus Christ,
   the only Son of God,
   eternally begotten of the Father,
   God from God, Light from Light,
   true God from true God,
   begotten, not made,
   of one Being with the Father;
   through him all things were made.
   For us and for our salvation
   he came down from heaven,
   was incarnate of the Holy Spirit and the Virgin Mary
   and became truly human.
   For our sake he was crucified under Pontius Pilate;
   he suffered death and was buried.
   On the third day he rose again
   in accordance with the Scriptures;
   he ascended into heaven
   and is seated at the right hand of the Father.
   He will come again in glory
   to judge the living and the dead,
   and his kingdom will have no end.

We believe in the Holy Spirit, the Lord, the giver of life,
   who proceeds from the Father (and the Son),**
   who with the Father and the Son
   is worshiped and glorified,
   who has spoken through the prophets.
   We believe in one holy catholic* and apostolic church.

We acknowledge one baptism
for the forgiveness of sins.

We look for the resurrection of the dead,
and the life of the world to come. Amen.

*Universal
** Roman Catholic and Protestant

A New Creation in Christ

"Therefore, if anyone is in Christ, the new creation has come: The old has gone, the new is here!" – 2 Corinthians 5:17 (NIV)

Renew your mind with the Word of God and be transformed. Confess the following ten affirmations of faith several times daily both silently and aloud with conviction.[1]

1. I am a new creation in Christ. (2 Cor. 5:17)

2. I am created by God in the womb. (Ps. 139:13–16)

3. I am called of God by name. (Isa. 43:1; 49:1)

4. I am forgiven and healed. (Ps. 103:3, 12)

5. I am God's child, born again of the incorruptible seed of the Word of God. (1 Pet. 2:2).

6. I am loved with an everlasting love. (Jer. 31:3)

7. I am washed, justified, and sanctified. (1 Cor. 6:11)

8. I know my old person is crucified and the body of sin is destroyed. (Rom. 6:6)

9. I am free from the works of the devil. They have been destroyed by Jesus – 1 Jn. 3:8

10. I am a partaker of the divine nature. (2 Pet. 1:4)

1. For nearly 400 more affirmations of faith see Peter Bellini, *Truth Therapy,* Chapter 7 "Confessing Our Faith: Affirmations."

Bibliography

Alexander, Paul. *Signs and Wonders: Why Pentecostalism is the World's Fastest Growing Faith*. San Francisco: Josey-Bass, 2009.

Allen, Paul. *Ernan McMullin and Critical Realism in the Science–Theology Dialogue*. London: Routledge, 2016.

Antiochian Orthodox Christian Archdiocese. *Pocket Prayer Book for Orthodox Christians 7th edition*. Englewood, NJ: Antiochian Orthodox Christian Archdiocese of North America, 1956.

Augsburger, David W. *Helping People Forgive*. Louisville, KY: Westminster John Knox, 1996.

Barbour, Ian G. *Religion and Science: Historical and Contemporary Issues*. San Francisco: HarperCollins, 1997.

Bainbridge, William Sims. *The Sociology of Religious Movements*. London: Routledge, 1997.

———. *When Science Meets Religion: Enemies, Strangers, or Partners?* New York: HarperCollins, 2000.

Bellini, Peter J. *Truth Therapy*. Eugene, OR: Wipf and Stock, 2014.

Brooke, John Hedley. *Science and Religion: Some Historical Perspectives*. Cambridge: Cambridge University Press, 1991.

Brown, Candy Gunther. *Testing Prayer: Science and Healing*. Cambridge, MA: Harvard University Press, 2012.

Chalmers, David. *The Conscious Mind*. Oxford: Oxford University Press, 1997.

Churchland, Paul. "Eliminative Materialism and the Propositional Attitudes." In *Philosophy of Mind: A Guide and Anthology*, edited by John Heil, 382–400. Oxford: Oxford Press, 2004.

Clark, Randy. *Eyewitness to Miracles: Watching the Gospel Come to Life*. Nashville: Thomas Nelson, 2018.

———. *The Biblical Guidebook to Deliverance*. Lake Mary, FL: Charisma, 2015.

Clayton, Philip. *Adventures in the Spirit: God, World, Divine Action*. Minneapolis: Fortress, 2008.

Clayton, Philip, and Paul Davies. *The Re-emergence of Emergence: The Emergentist Hypothesis from Science to Religion*. Oxford: Oxford University Press, 2008.

Collins, James. *Exorcism and Deliverance Ministry in the Twentieth Century*. Eugene, OR: Wipf and Stock, 2009.

Dauton-Fear, Andrew. *Healing in the Early Church, The Church's Ministry of Healing and Exorcism from the First to the Fifth Century.* Eugene, OR: Wipf and Stock, 2009.

"Emergence." *International Encyclopedia of Philosophy: A Peer-Reviewed Academic Resource.* https://www.iep.utm.edu/emergenc/.

Forcen, Carlos Espi. "St. Francis of Assisi: An Exorcist of Demons." *Journal of Humanistic Psychiatry,* 1:1, (2013) 5.

Forcen, Carlos Espi. and Fernando Espi Forcen. "Demonic Possessions and Mental Illness: Discussion of Selected Cases in Late Medieval Hagiographical Literature." *Early Science and Medicine,* 19:3, (2014) 258–279.

Foster, Richard. *Celebration of Discipline.* San Francisco: HarperCollins, 1988.

Foucault, Michel. *Madness and Civilization: A History of Insanity in the Age of Reason.* NY: Vintage, 1988.

Free, Michael. *CBT and Christianity: Strategies and Resources for Reconciling Faith and Therapy.* Hoboken, NJ: Wiley-Blackwell, 2015.

Gurnall, William. *The Christian in Complete Armor, reprint edition.* Peabody, MA: Hendrickson, 2010.

Jennings, Daniel R. *The Supernatural Occurrences of John Wesley.* Scotts Valley, CA: CreateSpace, 2012.

Johnsen, TJ, and O Friborg. "The Effects of Cognitive Behavioral Therapy as an Anti-depressive Treatment is Falling: A Meta-analysis." *Psychological Bulletin.* 141:4 (July, 2010) 747–768.

Johnson, Eric, ed. *Psychology and Christianity: Five Views.* Downers Grove, IL: IVP Academic, 2010.

Jokić-Begić, Nataša. "Cognitive-Behavioral Therapy and Neuroscience: Towards Closer Integration." *Psychological Topics* 19:2 (2010) 235–54.

Jones, Gregory L. *Embodying Forgiveness.* Grand Rapids: Eerdmans, 1995.

Kant, Immanuel. *Critique of Pure Reason.* Scotts Valley, CA: CreateSpace, 2010.

Keener, Craig. *Miracles: The Credibility of the New Testament Accounts, two vols.* Grand Rapids: Baker, 2011.

Kim, Jaegwon. *Supervenience and Mind: Selected Philosophical Essays.* Cambridge: Cambridge University Press, 1993.

———. "The Metaphysics of Reduction." In *Philosophy of Mind: A Guide and Anthology* edited by John Heil, 726–48. Oxford: Oxford Press, 2004.

Kraft, Charles H. *Christianity with Power: Your Worldview and Your Experience of the Supernatural.* Eugene, OR: Wipf and Stock, 2005.

Lindbeck, George. *The Nature of Doctrine: Religion and Theology in a Postliberal Age.* Louisville, KY: Westminster John Knox, 1984.

Lynch, D., et al. "Cognitive Behavioral Therapy for Major Psychiatric Disorder: Does it Really Work? A Meta-analytical Review of Well-controlled Trials." *Psychological Medicine Med.* 40:1 (2010) 9–24.

Madden, Deborah. *Inward and Outward Health: John Wesley's Holistic Concept of Medical Science, the Environment and Holy Living.* Eugene, OR: Wipf and Stock, 2012.

Maddox, Randy L. "John Wesley on Holistic Health and Healing," *Methodist History* 46:1 (October, 2007) 4–33.

Maddox, Randy L., and Jason Vickers, eds. *The Cambridge Companion to John Wesley*. Cambridge: Cambridge University Press, 2009.

McEnvoy, J.P., and Oscar Zarate. *Introducing Quantum Theory: A Graphic Guide*. London: Icon, 2014.

National Institute of Mental Health. "Any Anxiety Order Among Adults." *National Institute of Health*. http://www.nimh.nih.gov/health/statistics/prevalence/any-anxiety-disorder-among-adults.shtml.

———. "Any Mental Illness Among U.S. Adults." http://www.nimh.nih.gov/health/statistics/prevalence/any-mental-illness-ami-among-adults.shtml.

———. "Leading Cause of Death Ages 18-65 in the U.S." http://www.nimh.nih.gov/health/statistics/suicide/leading-causes-of-death-ages-18-65-in-the-us.shtml.

———. "U.S. Leading Categories of Diseases/Disorders." http://www.nimh.nih.gov/health/statistics/disability/us-leading-categories-of-diseases-disorders.shtml.

———. "Suicide in America: Frequently Asked Questions." http://www.nimh.nih.gov/health/topics/suicide-prevention/index.shtml.

O'Connor, Timothy, and Hong Yu Wong. "Emergent Properties." *Stanford Encyclopedia of Philosophy*, Edited by Edward N. Zalta. Summer 2015 Edition. https://plato.stanford.edu/archives/sum2015/entries/properties-emergent/.

Outler, Albert, ed. *The Works of John Wesley*. Nashville: Abingdon, 1986.

Padgett, Alan G., and J.B. Stump, eds. *The Blackwell Companion to Science and Christianity*. Hoboken, NJ: Wiley-Blackwell, 2012.

Paneck, Richard. *The 4 Percent Universe: Dark Matter, Dark Energy, and the Race to Discover the Rest of Reality*. New York: Mariner, 2011.

Peacocke, Arthur. *Theology for a Scientific Age: Being and Becoming-Natural, Divine, and Human*. Minneapolis: Fortress, 1993.

Pearce, Michelle. *Cognitive Behavioral Therapy for Christians with Depression: A Practical Tool-Based Primer*. West Conshohocken, PA: Templeton, 2016.

Polanyi, Michael. *Personal Knowledge: Toward a Post-Critical Philosophy*. Chicago: University of Chicago Press, 1974.

Polkinghorne, John. *Science and Religion in Quest of Truth*. New Haven: Yale University Press, 2011.

Rio, Knut, et al., eds. *Pentecostalism and Witchcraft: Spiritual Warfare in African and Melanesia*. London: Palgrave Macmillan, 2017.

Russell, Robert J., et al. *Quantum Mechanics: Scientific Perspective on Divine Action Volume 5*. Vatican Observatory and Center for Theology, 2002.

Russell, Robert J. "Dialogue, Science and Theology" in the *Interdisciplinary Encyclopedia of Religion and Science*, Edited by G. Tanzella-Nitti and A. Strauma. http://inters.org/dialogue-science-theology. 2002.

Sandford, John Loren, and Mark Sandford. *Deliverance and Inner Healing*. Grand Rapids: Baker, 2008.

Schultz., F. LeRon. *Reforming Theological Anthropology: After the Philosophical Turn to Relationality.* Grand Rapids: Eerdmans, 2003.

Smietana, Bob. "Mental Illness Remains Taboo Topic for Many Pastors." LifeWay Research. https://lifewayresearch.com/2014/09/22/mental-illness-remains-taboo-topic-for-many-pastors/. 2014.

Thepohan the Recluse. *The Path to Salvation: A Manual of Spiritual Transformation.* Translated by Seraphim Rose. Safford, AZ: St. Paiusius Monastery, 1996.

Twelfttree, Graham H. *In the Name of Jesus: Exorcism Among Early Christians.* Grand Rapids: Baker, 2007

———. *Jesus the Exorcist: A Contribution to the Study of The Historical Jesus.* Eugene, OR: Wipf and Stock, 2011.

Tyerman, L., *The Life and Times of Rev. John Wesley, M.A.* London: Hodder and Stoughton, 1870.

Webster, Robert. *Methodism and the Miraculous: John Wesley's Idea of the Supernatural and the Identification of Methodists in the Eighteenth-Century.* Lexington, KY: Emeth, 2013.

Worthington, Everett, L., Jr., ed. *Dimensions of Forgiveness: Psychological Research and Theological Perspectives.* Philadelphia: Templeton Foundation, 1998.

Index